AMERICAN
Phrasal Verbs
for Immigrants

CONTENTS

Hold on Knock down **Walk around** Weird out **Break up** Pull off
Buckle up Dish out **Stick up for** Turn in **Drop by** Slip away
Wash up Lash out **Sink in** Play along **Get ahead** Run out **Hop in**
Cut back **Think through** Pop out **Beat up** Take away **Kick out**
Blend in **Head up** Blurt out **Rely on** Suck up to **Reason with**
Show off **Back up** Go along with **Max out** Buy into **Slip up**
Get back at **Kick in** Burn out **Put up to** Lay off **Break in** Rat out
Shake up Act out **Settle in** Go ahead **Butter up** Come off **Pop in**
Stay away **Go down** Chip in **Step out** Step up **Cool off** Put in
Seek out Bail on **Bring down** Set up **Cheat on** Live up to
Bounce back Cheese off **Go for** Feel down **Get rid of** Wrap up
Talk into Hammer out **Follow up** Back down **Waltz in** Fit in
Talk up Hash out **Go under** Be into **Get at** Take up with **Set back**
Drift apart **Buckle down**

Feel for **Rile up** Live off **Run into** Level with **Size up** Pull out
Talk down to Swing by **Fill up on** Come around **Look past**
Crank up **Fight back** Slip out **Rule out** Manage to **Bottle up**
Mooch off **Iron out** Weigh in **Set off** Bump up **Lay on** Mess with
Turn up Sleep in **Throw in** Come out **Tip off** Step in **Root for**
Poke around **Set aside** End up **Pile on** Stumble upon **Be onto**
Draw up **Cap off** Pop up **Talk down** Bust in **Draw out** Round up
Sponge off Amp up **Prop up** Sniff around **Luck out** Peer out
Eat away Plop down **Shy away** Ponder over **Home in on**
Hone in on **Wise up** Lawyer up **Heat up** Opt in **See in** Look in
Sit in Turn in **Opt out** See out **Watch out** Click out **Wash out**

Dump out **Pour out** Set out **Let out** Keep out **Clip on** Add on
Cheer on Sleep on **Keep on** Drag on

Unit5 Page 219

Take on Leave on **Press on** Run on **Work on** Egg on **Nod off**
Tick off **Live off** Call off **Pay off** Lay off **Trade off** Push off
Show off Set off **Let off** Go off **Dry off** Fight off **Look after**
Take after **Run around** Chase after **Go after** Get after
Come before Put before **Go before** Close down **Wear down**
Track down **Tear down** Run down **Narrow down** Let down
Keep down Crack down on **Cut down** Hold down **Hold out for**
Hold back from **Rip up** Sign up **Mix up** Clog up **Tape up** Lace up
Hike up Set up **Clear up** Wrap up **Work up** Turn up **Run up**
Make up **Hand over** Knock over **Look over** Run over **Stop over**
Turn over **Sleep over** Take over **Make over** Go over **Skip over**
Come under **Fall under** Put under **Go under** Pass through
Break through Fall through

Unit6 Page 273

Get through with Go through with **Pull through** Skim through
Tack on Pile on **Try on** Decide on **Cheat on** Lie on **Come on**
Count on **Bank on** Go back on **Have on** Touch on **Come up with**
Go through **Pick up** Put off **Look up** Take off **Put down**
Put up with **Make up** Turn down **Fall off** Fall apart **Wander off**
Sit out **Point out** Blend in **Jump ahead** Put aside **Set aside**
Turn up **Get away with** Take in **Take over** Bring up **Take out on**
Fill in **Put on** Fake out **Run out of** Take back **Work out**
Come across **Look after** Put together **Put through** Hold on
Look into Come back **Call on** Carry on **Come up** Work on

Slack off Drop off **Come out** Look out **Turn off** Take away
Make out Look up to **Turn in** Hand in **Pass out** Run into **Put up**
Carry out **Grow into** Grow out **Drop out** Flunk out **Turn out**
Fall back on **Fall behind** Look around **Pull off** Come to
Make do with Hang up **Pounce on** Join in **Result in** Succeed in
Engage in Cave in **Bring in** Fall in

Unit7 Page 341

Zero in on Check in **Check out** Check on **Log in** Log out
Get on with Settle on **Seize on** Bring on **Focus on** Insist on
Catch on Clock off **Clock out** Punch in **Punch out** Dash off
Doze off Ease off **Get off** Head off **Log off** Reel off **Tell off**
Wear off **Wipe off** Write off **Block off** Break off **Come off**
Back out **Call out** Clear out **Die out** Fall out **Farm out** Hear out
Help out Leave out **Miss out on** Sort out **Speak out** Block up
Brighten up Burn up **Call up** Check up on **Chop up** Close up
Crack up Do up **Dress up** Eat up **Go up** Fix up **Hold up** Hurry up
Keep up Screw up **Warm up** Wake up **Go along with**
Grind along **Happen along** Move along **Muddle along**
Pass along **Play along** Run along **String along** Tag along
Take along Trundle along **Be along** Stroll through **Plonk down**
Curse out **Run by** Pass away **Act up** Big up

Unit 1

Find out

To discover or obtain information about something.

*I need to **find out** the time of the meeting.*

*Can you help me **find out** who called me?*

*I'll **find out** the answer and let you know.*

*We need to **find out** where the nearest gas station is.*

*The detective worked hard to **find out** the truth about the case.*

Get along

To have a harmonious relationship or friendship with someone.

*We always **get along** well despite our differences.*

*It's important for colleagues to **get along** in the workplace.*

*Do you **get along** with your new neighbors?*

*We need to **get along** if we're going to work together.*

*Despite their contrasting personalities, they manage to **get along** brilliantly.*

Cheer up

To become happier or to make someone feel happier.

*His favorite song always helps **cheer up** his mood.*

*Why don't you watch a funny movie to **cheer up**?*

*I brought you some flowers to **cheer you up**.*

*Try to **cheer up**; things will get better.*

*She sent a funny meme to **cheer up** her friend.*

Pick up

To lift something or someone from a surface; to acquire or gather something.

*Can you help me **pick up** these books from the floor?*

*He needs to **pick up** his dry cleaning on the way home.*

*I'll **pick you up** from the airport at 6 PM.*

*Let's **pick up** some groceries on our way back.*

*She always forgets to **pick up** her room before guests arrive.*

Drop off

To deliver or leave someone or something at a destination.

*I'll **drop off** the package at your office on my way home.*

*Can you **drop me off** at the train station?*

*The school bus will **drop off** the kids at the front gate.*

*We need to **drop off** these clothes at the donation center.*

*Let me know if you need a **drop-off** after the event.*

Look for

To search for or seek something.

*I need to **look for** my keys; I can't find them anywhere.*

*Can you help me **look for** a good restaurant in the area?*

*She is **looking for** a job in marketing.*

*Let's **look for** the missing piece of the puzzle together.*

*We'll need to **look for** a solution to this problem.*

Figure out

To understand, solve, or find a solution to a problem.

*I need some time to **figure out** how to fix this issue.*

*Can you **figure out** the answer to this riddle?*

*We need to **figure out** a plan for the project.*

*It took a while to **figure out** the new software.*

*She finally managed to **figure out** the math problem.*

Move in

To begin living in a new residence.

*We will **move in** to our new house next week.*

*They decided to **move in** together after getting engaged.*

*Did you hear that the Smiths are planning to **move in** next door?*

*It's always exciting to **move in** and start a new chapter.*

*They're helping us **move in** our furniture this weekend.*

Move out

To leave a residence and go live somewhere else.

*We decided to **move out** of the city and into the suburbs.*

*After graduation, many students choose to **move out** and live on their own.*

*They're planning to **move out** of their apartment next month.*

*It's a big decision to **move out** and live independently.*

*We helped them **move out** of their old house last weekend.*

Hang out

To spend time together in a casual or relaxed manner.

*We used to **hang out** at the park every weekend.*

*Let's **hang out** at the coffee shop after work.*

*They often **hang out** with friends on Friday nights.*

*We should **hang out** and catch up sometime.*

*During the summer, we like to **hang out** by the pool.*

Bring up

To mention or introduce a topic in conversation.

*Don't **bring up** that sensitive issue during the family dinner.*

*She always finds a way to **bring up** interesting topics in meetings.*

*Why did you have to **bring up** the past again?*

*It's important to **bring up** concerns in a respectful manner.*

*Let's **bring up** this matter at the next team meeting.*

Piss off

To make someone angry or irritated.

*His rude comments really **pissed off** his colleagues.*

*Don't intentionally **piss off** your customers; it's bad for business.*

*She was **pissed off** when she found out about the mistake.*

*It's best not to **piss off** your boss before the performance review.*

*He tends to **piss off** everyone with his sarcastic remarks.*

Calm down

To become or make someone less agitated, anxious, or angry.

*You need to **calm down** before discussing this issue.*

*Deep breaths can help you **calm down** in stressful situations.*

*She tried to **calm down** the upset child with a soothing lullaby.*

*It's essential to **calm down** after a heated argument.*

*He needed a moment to **calm down** before making a decision.*

Turn out

To end up or result in a particular way.

*The party **turned out** to be a great success.*

*Despite initial doubts, the project **turned out** exceptionally well.*

*How did the experiment **turn out**? Any interesting findings?*

*It's amazing how things can **turn out** differently than expected.*

*Despite the challenges, everything **turned out** better than we thought.*

Mess up

To make a mistake or to ruin something.

> *I accidentally **messed up** the order; I'm so sorry.*

> *It's easy to **mess up** when you're working under pressure.*

> *Try not to **mess up** the presentation; it's crucial for the client.*

> *She felt terrible after realizing she **messed up** the important document.*

> *It's okay to make mistakes; the important thing is to learn from them and not **mess up** again.*

Fool around

To engage in aimless or playful behavior, often in a light-hearted manner.

> *They like to **fool around** during their break time at work.*

> *Stop **fooling around** and focus on your homework.*

> *It's important not to **fool around** when handling serious tasks.*

*They spent the afternoon **fooling around** in the park.*

*It's fine to **fool around** as long as you get your work done on time.*

Come over

To visit someone's residence or location.

*Feel free to **come over** for coffee anytime.*

*Can you **come over** and help me with this heavy lifting?*

*We're planning to **come over** to your place for dinner next week.*

*She asked if she could **come over** and borrow some books.*

*Don't hesitate to **come over** if you need assistance.*

Catch up

To reach the same level or status as others; to informally converse with someone to learn about recent events.

*I need to **catch up** with my classmates on the latest assignments.*

*Let's grab lunch and **catch up** on what's been happening in our lives.*

*It's essential to **catch up** on industry trends to stay competitive.*

*After being away, she wanted to **catch up** with her family and friends.*

*We should schedule a meeting to **catch up** on the project's progress.*

Call off

To cancel or abandon a planned event or activity.

*We had to **call off** the picnic due to bad weather.*

*They decided to **call off** the meeting because of scheduling conflicts.*

*Due to unforeseen circumstances, they had to **call***

off the wedding.

It's disappointing when you have to **call off** a trip at the last minute.

We might need to **call off** the event if not enough people confirm their attendance.

Deal with

To handle, cope with, or address a situation or problem.

She knows how to **deal with** difficult customers calmly.

We need to find a way to **deal with** the increasing workload.

He's experienced in **dealing with** challenging negotiations.

It's important to **deal with** stress in a healthy way.

We'll have a meeting to discuss how to **deal with** the unexpected changes.

Take over

To assume control or responsibility for something.

> The new manager will **take over** the team starting next month.

> After the retirement, his successor will **take over** the company.

> They plan to **take over** the market with their innovative product.

> The military decided to **take over** the operation to ensure its success.

> The young entrepreneur aims to **take over** the tech industry.

Bust on

To tease or make fun of someone in a playful manner.

> It's common for friends to **bust on** each other for a good laugh.

> He likes to **bust on** his colleagues in a friendly way during breaks.

*Don't take it seriously; they're just **busting on** you because they like you.*

*We used to **bust on** each other in high school all the time.*

*It's all in good fun; they only **bust on** people they like.*

Cut off

To disconnect or stop the flow of something.

*We had to **cut off** the water supply temporarily for repairs.*

*His phone call was **cut off** abruptly due to poor reception.*

*If you don't pay the bill, they might **cut off** your electricity.*

*The road was **cut off** due to heavy snowfall.*

*We had to **cut off** the discussion to attend an urgent meeting.*

Set up

To establish or arrange something.

> They helped **set up** the stage for the concert.

> We need to **set up** a meeting to discuss the project details.

> He decided to **set up** his own business after gaining experience.

> She helped him **set up** his profile on the dating app.

> The team worked together to **set up** the exhibition in record time.

Pull over

To move a vehicle to the side of the road and stop.

> The police officer signaled for him to **pull over** for a routine check.

> She needed to **pull over** and ask for directions.

> The driver decided to **pull over** and take a break from the long drive.

*It's important to **pull over** if you're feeling drowsy while driving.*

*The car had a flat tire, so they had to **pull over** to change it.*

Dig in

To enthusiastically begin eating; to get involved or work hard on something.

*Once the food was served, everyone was eager to **dig in**.*

*They decided to **dig in** and complete the project ahead of schedule.*

*It's time to **dig in** and focus on finishing the assignment.*

*As soon as the cake was cut, the kids started to **dig in** with delight.*

*She encouraged her team to **dig in** and give their best effort.*

Hold back

To restrain or keep from progressing.

> *She had to **hold back** tears when saying goodbye.*

> *Don't **hold back** your opinions during the discussion; we want to hear them.*

> *It's difficult to **hold back** excitement when receiving good news.*

> *He had to **hold back** his laughter during the serious meeting.*

> *It's important not to **hold back** progress; embrace change.*

Come up

To arise or occur; to suggest or think of; to approach or move closer.

> *We didn't expect that issue to **come up** during the presentation.*

> *They need to **come up** with a solution to the problem as soon as possible.*

*Can you **come up** to the front and share your ideas with the team?*

*Unexpected expenses **came up** during the renovation project.*

*As the deadline **comes up**, we need to finalize our plans.*

Work out

To exercise; to resolve; to develop successfully.

*I try to **work out** at the gym three times a week.*

*Let's sit down and discuss how we can **work out** this issue.*

*She hopes the new plan will **work out** for the company's benefit.*

*We need to **work out** the details before launching the project.*

*Exercising regularly can help you **work out** stress and stay healthy.*

Go over

To review, examine, or discuss in detail.

> *Let's **go over** the main points of the presentation before the meeting.*

> *He decided to **go over** the contract one more time before signing it.*

> *We need to **go over** the budget to ensure we're on track.*

> *They scheduled a meeting to **go over** the project's progress and challenges.*

> *Take some time to **go over** your notes before the exam.*

Get over

To recover from or move beyond a difficult or emotional experience.

> *It took him a while to **get over** the loss of his pet.*

> *She needs time to **get over** the breakup and heal.*

> *He managed to **get over** the disappointment and*

focus on the future.

*It's essential to **get over** setbacks and keep moving forward.*

*With support, she was able to **get over** the trauma and rebuild her life.*

Pass out

To lose consciousness; to distribute or give something to others.

*She felt dizzy and almost **passed out** during the intense workout.*

*The heat was so overwhelming that several people **passed out** at the outdoor event.*

*After a long day, he **passed out** on the couch from exhaustion.*

*They decided to **pass out** flyers to promote the upcoming event.*

*He didn't expect the news to be so shocking that he almost **passed out**.*

Hook up

To connect or link; to engage in a casual sexual encounter.

> *They plan to **hook up** the new sound system to the TV for better audio.*

> *She didn't want to **hook up** emotionally, just enjoy a casual relationship.*

> *Can you help me **hook up** my laptop to the projector for the presentation?*

> *They decided to **hook up** for a night of fun without any commitments.*

> *He spent the weekend trying to **hook up** the new gaming console to the TV.*

Turn down

To decrease the volume, intensity, or level of something; to reject an offer or invitation.

> *Can you **turn down** the music? It's too loud.*

> *She had to **turn down** the job offer due to personal reasons.*

*He decided to **turn down** the heat to make the room more comfortable.*

*It's not easy to **turn down** an opportunity that comes once in a lifetime.*

*She politely **turned down** the invitation as she had prior commitments.*

Tag along

To accompany someone, often without a specific invitation.

*He asked if he could **tag along** to the movie with us.*

*She decided to **tag along** to the business meeting to observe.*

*Feel free to **tag along** if you want to join us for lunch.*

*He didn't mind if his little brother wanted to **tag along** to the party.*

*She didn't have plans, so she decided to **tag along** on the hiking trip.*

Ask out

To invite someone on a date or social outing.

> *He mustered the courage to finally **ask out** his crush.*

> *She was thrilled when he decided to **ask her out** for coffee.*

> *After getting to know her, he decided to **ask her out** to dinner.*

> *It's nerve-wracking to **ask someone out**, but it's worth the risk.*

> *They met at a party, and he gathered the courage to **ask her out** the next day.*

Give in

To surrender, yield, or relent; to accept defeat or a demand.

> *After a long argument, he decided to **give in** and apologize.*

> *It's important to stand firm on your principles and not **give in** easily.*

*She was persistent, and he eventually **gave in** to her request.*

*It's hard to **give in** when you believe strongly in your position.*

*He didn't want to argue any longer, so he chose to **give in** and find a compromise.*

Look forward to

To anticipate or feel excited about a future event or situation.

*They **look forward to** spending the holidays with family and friends.*

*She **looks forward to** the weekend as a break from work.*

*Everyone **looks forward to** the annual company retreat.*

*He **looks forward to** the opportunity to travel and explore new places.*

*We **look forward to** celebrating your achievements at the upcoming ceremony.*

Barge in

To enter abruptly or forcefully without permission; to interrupt.

*He didn't mean to **barge in** on their private conversation.*

*She accidentally **barged in** on the meeting without realizing it was in progress.*

*It's rude to **barge in** on someone's office without knocking first.*

*He didn't want to **barge in**, so he waited for a break in the conversation.*

*It's important to respect privacy and not **barge in** on someone's personal space.*

Storm out

To leave angrily or abruptly, often as a reaction to a disagreement or frustration.

*After the argument, he chose to **storm out** of the room without saying a word.*

She couldn't handle the criticism and decided to

storm out of the meeting.

*He tends to **storm out** when things don't go his way.*

*It's better to take a moment to cool off than to **storm out** in the heat of the moment.*

*They watched as she angrily **stormed out** of the restaurant.*

Warm up

To increase in temperature; to prepare the body for physical activity.

*Before exercising, it's important to **warm up** to prevent injuries.*

*She decided to **warm up** by doing some light stretches before the run.*

*Can you help me **warm up** the soup before serving it?*

*The athlete spent a few minutes doing cardio to **warm up** before the competition.*

*Let's **warm up** by jogging around the park before*

starting the workout.

Dive in/into

To start or engage in something enthusiastically or without hesitation.

*She decided to **dive into** the new project with full commitment.*

*It's time to **dive into** the world of learning and exploration.*

*He couldn't wait to **dive into** the exciting book he just bought.*

*Let's **dive in** and tackle the challenging tasks together.*

*They encouraged the team to **dive into** the creative process with passion.*

Put down

To place something on a surface; to criticize or belittle someone; to euthanize an animal.

*Can you please **put down** the grocery bags on the table?*

*It's not right to **put down** others just to make yourself feel superior.*

*She had to make the difficult decision to **put down** her ailing pet.*

*Let's **put down** our thoughts on paper before discussing them.*

*It's important to provide constructive feedback rather than **putting down** your colleagues.*

Look up

To search for information; to admire or respect someone; to improve or become brighter.

*If you don't know the definition, you can **look it up** in the dictionary.*

*She has always **looked up to** her older sister as a role model.*

*The weather seems to be **looking up** after a week of rain.*

*Before the meeting, he decided to **look up** some relevant statistics.*

*He asked me to **look up** the address on the internet.*

Roll over

To turn one's body to face a different direction; to defer or postpone a financial investment.

*He couldn't sleep well, so he decided to **roll over** in bed.*

*It's time to **roll over** your 401(k) to maximize your retirement savings.*

*The dog likes to **roll over** and play dead during tricks.*

*She asked the financial advisor about the best time to **roll over** her investments.*

*After waking up, he tends to **roll over** and check his phone for messages.*

Come down with

To become ill with a specific illness or condition.

> She started to feel unwell and feared she might **come down with** the flu.

> He realized he might **come down with** a cold after being exposed to the virus.

> If you **come down with** symptoms, it's important to seek medical advice.

> After spending time in the rain, he began to **come down with** a fever.

> She decided to rest at home to avoid **coming down with** the contagious illness.

Name after

To give a person or thing a name in honor of or to resemble another.

> They chose to **name their daughter after** the grandmother who passed away.

> He decided to **name the new product after** his favorite childhood toy.

*The city was **named after** a famous historical figure.*

*Many celebrities **name their children after** influential people in their lives.*

*They decided to **name the street after** the local hero who made significant contributions.*

Come across

To encounter or find unexpectedly; to be perceived in a particular way.

*While hiking, they **came across** a beautiful waterfall in the forest.*

*He **came across** an old photograph while cleaning out the attic.*

*She always **comes across** as confident during presentations.*

*During the road trip, they **came across** a charming small town.*

*He didn't mean to **come across** as rude; it was a misunderstanding.*

Bum out

To disappoint or make someone feel upset or sad.

*It really **bummed him out** when his favorite team lost the game.*

*Don't let a small setback **bum you out**; there's always a way to bounce back.*

*She tried not to let the bad news **bum her out** for too long.*

*It can **bum us out** when plans don't go as expected, but there's always another opportunity.*

*He didn't want to **bum out** the atmosphere, so he kept a positive attitude despite challenges.*

Settle down

To establish a permanent residence; to calm down or become less active.

*After years of traveling, he decided it was time to **settle down** and start a family.*

*It's important to **settle down** before making important life decisions.*

*She needed some time to **settle down** after the hectic workweek.*

*They chose a quiet neighborhood to **settle down** and raise their children.*

*As they reached retirement, they decided to **settle down** in a peaceful countryside home.*

Stop by

To make a brief visit or stop at a location.

*Feel free to **stop by** my office if you have any questions.*

*We'll **stop by** the grocery store on our way home.*

*He decided to **stop by** the café for a cup of coffee.*

*Can you **stop by** the pharmacy and pick up my prescription?*

*It's always nice when friends **stop by** unexpectedly.*

Stand up

To rise to a standing position; to support or defend someone or something.

> *When the teacher enters the room, everyone should **stand up** as a sign of respect.*
>
> *It's important to **stand up** for what you believe in, even in challenging situations.*
>
> *He decided to **stand up** against the injustice he witnessed.*
>
> *She asked for volunteers to **stand up** and share their opinions.*
>
> *If you're being mistreated, it's crucial to **stand up** for yourself.*

Blow off

To ignore or dismiss; to cancel plans without prior notice.

> *He tends to **blow off** important emails, which can lead to misunderstandings.*
>
> *She decided to **blow off** the invitation and stay*

home instead.

*It's not polite to **blow off** someone who is genuinely trying to help.*

*They agreed not to **blow off** their commitment to the project.*

*He apologized for having to **blow off** the meeting due to a sudden emergency.*

Make up

To reconcile after a disagreement; to create or invent; to apply cosmetics.

*After their argument, they decided to **make up** and move forward.*

*She loves to **make up** stories to entertain her younger siblings.*

*It's important to **make up** with friends after a misunderstanding.*

*She took a few minutes to **make up** before going on stage.*

*They decided to **make up** for lost time by*

spending the weekend together.

Carry on

To continue doing something; to proceed or persist.

> *Despite the challenges, they decided to **carry on** with the project.*

> *It's important to **carry on** with your goals even in the face of setbacks.*

> *After a brief pause, the meeting will **carry on** as scheduled.*

> *She encouraged her team to **carry on** with their hard work and dedication.*

> *Despite the criticism, they chose to **carry on** with their innovative approach.*

Come up with

To devise, create, or produce (an idea, plan, solution, etc.).

> *She managed to **come up with** a brilliant*

solution to the complex problem.

*They brainstormed for hours to **come up with** a creative marketing campaign.*

*It's challenging to **come up with** innovative ideas under tight deadlines.*

*He always has a way to **come up with** unique and interesting concepts.*

*Despite the constraints, they were able to **come up with** a viable business plan.*

Kick off

To start or initiate; to begin a project, event, or activity.

*The company will **kick off** the new year with a team-building retreat.*

*They plan to **kick off** the conference with an inspiring keynote speaker.*

*Let's **kick off** the project with a comprehensive planning session.*

*The concert will **kick off** with a performance by a*

*They decided to **kick off** the campaign with a series of engaging social media posts.*

Put aside

To save or reserve for future use; to set aside or ignore temporarily.

*It's important to **put aside** some money each month for unexpected expenses.*

*They agreed to **put aside** their differences and work towards a common goal.*

*She decided to **put aside** some time each day for personal relaxation.*

*Let's **put aside** the disagreement for now and focus on the task at hand.*

*He chose to **put aside** his personal feelings to support his friend's decision.*

Screw over

To betray or deceive someone; to treat unfairly or

dishonestly.

> He felt deeply hurt when his close friend tried to **screw him over** in the business deal.

> It's important to be cautious and not allow others to **screw you over** in negotiations.

> She realized her business partner was attempting to **screw her over** by taking credit for her ideas.

> They vowed never to **screw over** their employees by cutting corners on safety.

> It's crucial to build trust in relationships and not **screw over** those who depend on you.

Look out

To be cautious or aware of potential danger; to watch or pay attention.

> While crossing the street, always **look out** for oncoming traffic.

> He warned his friends to **look out** for signs of suspicious activity in the neighborhood.

> It's essential to **look out** for each other's well-

being in a close-knit community.

*As a team, they agreed to **look out** for any challenges that might arise during the project.*

*Parents often remind their children to **look out** for potential dangers in unfamiliar places.*

Watch out

To be cautious or vigilant; to be aware of potential danger.

*When crossing the street, always **watch out** for oncoming traffic.*

*She warned her friends to **watch out** for slippery surfaces in the rainy weather.*

*It's important to **watch out** for signs of exhaustion during strenuous physical activity.*

*He advised them to **watch out** for potential scams when making online transactions.*

*While hiking, they were told to **watch out** for wildlife in the area.*

Count on

To rely on or trust someone or something; to depend on for support or assistance.

*You can always **count on** her to help in times of need.*

*They decided to **count on** each other's strengths to complete the project successfully.*

*It's reassuring to know you can **count on** your friends during challenging times.*

*He promised to **count on** their support as he embarked on a new endeavor.*

*They learned to **count on** the reliability of the team to meet deadlines.*

Stick around

To remain in a place; to stay or linger.

*Feel free to **stick around** after the meeting if you have any questions.*

*He decided to **stick around** the event to network with other professionals.*

*She asked her friends to **stick around** for a little while longer to chat.*

*Despite the challenges, they chose to **stick around** and find solutions together.*

*After the concert, some fans decided to **stick around** to meet the band.*

Unit   2

Take down

To remove or dismantle; to record information; to defeat or overcome.

*They needed a ladder to **take down** the decorations after the party.*

*He used a notebook to **take down** important points during the meeting.*

*It's crucial to **take down** inaccurate information to prevent confusion.*

*They were determined to **take down** the reigning champions in the upcoming match.*

*She decided to **take down** her opponent with a strategic move in the chess game.*

Set on

To be determined to do something; to place or fix on something.

*She was **set on** pursuing a career in environmental conservation.*

*Despite the challenges, they remained **set on** achieving their goals.*

*He was **set on** breaking the record for the fastest marathon time.*

*They were **set on** making a positive impact in their community.*

*She remained **set on** her decision to travel and explore different cultures.*

Back off

To retreat or move away; to stop interfering or

asserting oneself.

> *When the dog growled, he quickly decided to **back off** to avoid any confrontation.*

> *She told her colleague to **back off** and let her handle the situation on her own.*

> *It's important to **back off** and give people space when they need it.*

> *He realized he needed to **back off** and allow his friend to make their own decisions.*

> *After the disagreement, they agreed to **back off** and give each other time to cool down.*

Flip out

To react with extreme excitement, anger, or surprise.

> *When he saw the surprise party, he couldn't help but **flip out** with joy.*

> *She tends to **flip out** when things don't go according to plan.*

> *He didn't expect the news to make her **flip out** in anger.*

*It's best to stay calm and not **flip out** in stressful situations.*

*They worried that revealing the truth might make him **flip out** with frustration.*

Take off

To remove or lift off; to leave quickly, especially by airplane; to become successful or popular.

*Before boarding the plane, passengers are instructed to **take off** their shoes.*

*They decided to **take off** for a spontaneous weekend getaway.*

*The new product began to **take off** in the market due to its innovative features.*

*As the rocket launched, everyone watched it **take off** into the sky.*

*She had to **take off** from the meeting early to catch a flight.*

Bump into

To unexpectedly encounter or meet someone; to collide with something or someone.

> *While shopping, she happened to **bump into** an old friend from college.*

> *He accidentally **bumped into** a lamppost while checking his phone.*

> *It's always a pleasant surprise to **bump into** familiar faces in a new city.*

> *She didn't expect to **bump into** her former coworker at the bookstore.*

> *They agreed to meet at the coffee shop but **bumped into** each other on the way there.*

Track down

To locate or find someone or something after searching or investigating.

> *The detective worked hard to **track down** the missing person.*

> *She managed to **track down** the rare book at a*

local bookstore.

They decided to hire a private investigator to **track down** *their long-lost relative.*

Despite the challenges, they were determined to **track down** *the stolen artwork.*

With the help of technology, they were able to **track down** *the origin of the mysterious phone call.*

Screw up

To make a mistake or mess up a situation.

She accidentally **screwed up** *the important presentation by mixing up the slides.*

It's okay to make mistakes; the important thing is to learn from them when you **screw up***.*

He didn't want to **screw up** *the recipe, so he followed it carefully.*

If you **screw up** *at work, it's crucial to take responsibility and fix the error.*

She felt disappointed after realizing she had

screwed up the job interview.

Drop in

To visit someone casually and without a prior appointment.

*Feel free to **drop in** for a cup of coffee whenever you're in the neighborhood.*

*She decided to **drop in** on her friend to catch up on the latest news.*

*If you're passing by, don't hesitate to **drop in** and say hello.*

*They were pleasantly surprised when their neighbors decided to **drop in** with a homemade pie.*

*He didn't expect his parents to **drop in** unannounced for a weekend visit.*

Put up

To place or hang something in a specific location; to accommodate or provide lodging.

*She decided to **put up** a new painting in the living room.*

*They offered to **put up** their guests in the spare bedroom for the night.*

*He helped **put up** decorations for the upcoming celebration.*

*It's time to **put up** the holiday lights outside the house.*

*Can you help me **put up** these posters around the campus?*

Point out

To indicate or draw attention to something; to mention or identify.

*During the presentation, he decided to **point out** the key features of the new product.*

*She gently **pointed out** the error in the report to her colleague.*

*It's important to **point out** potential risks before starting a new project.*

*He couldn't help but **point out** the beautiful sunset to everyone around him.*

*She wanted to **point out** the positive aspects of the situation despite the challenges.*

Come forward

To volunteer or offer help; to reveal oneself or one's identity.

*She decided to **come forward** and assist with the community project.*

*It took courage for him to **come forward** and share his personal experiences.*

*They encouraged witnesses to **come forward** and provide information about the incident.*

*If you have any ideas, feel free to **come forward** and share them with the team.*

*It's important for victims to feel safe when deciding to **come forward** and report incidents.*

Stand for

To represent or symbolize; to tolerate or support.

*The colors of the flag **stand for** the nation's history and values.*

*He refused to **stand for** unfair treatment and advocated for change.*

*They believed in principles that **stand for** equality and justice.*

*She wouldn't **stand for** any form of discrimination in her workplace.*

*As a leader, he wanted his actions to **stand for** integrity and accountability.*

Fill out

To complete a form or document by providing necessary information.

*Before the interview, please remember to **fill out** the application form.*

*They asked participants to **fill out** a brief survey about their experiences.*

It's essential to **fill out** the medical history form accurately for proper treatment.

She took a few minutes to **fill out** the feedback form after the training session.

He was instructed to **fill out** the online registration form for the upcoming event.

Fill in

To provide missing information or details; to act as a substitute or replacement.

She had to **fill in** the gaps in the report before submitting it to the supervisor.

He agreed to **fill in** for his colleague who was on vacation.

Can you please **fill in** the missing dates on the calendar?

They needed someone to **fill in** for the absent speaker at the conference.

It's essential to **fill in** the necessary details on the form to complete the registration process.

Jot down

To quickly write or note down information in a brief
and informal manner.

> *During the meeting, she liked to **jot down** key
> points for later reference.*

> *He used a small notebook to **jot down** ideas that
> came to him throughout the day.*

> *She asked him to **jot down** the contact details for
> future communication.*

> *It's helpful to **jot down** important tasks to
> remember them later.*

> *They encouraged students to **jot down** questions
> during the lecture for a Q&A session afterward.*

Pass on

To decline or refuse; to transmit or convey something
to the next person.

> *He decided to **pass on** the dessert after a filling
> meal.*

> *She chose to **pass on** the job offer and pursue*

other opportunities.

*It's important to **pass on** information accurately to avoid misunderstandings.*

*They agreed to **pass on** the responsibility to a more experienced team member.*

*Before the meeting, please check if anyone wants to **pass on** any agenda items.*

Grow up

To mature or age; to develop both physically and emotionally.

*She watched her children **grow up** into independent and responsible adults.*

*It's natural for teenagers to undergo challenges and changes as they **grow up**.*

*He hoped to **grow up** to be as successful as his role models.*

*They witnessed the neighborhood children **grow up** and graduate from school.*

*As individuals **grow up**, their perspectives and*

priorities often shift.

Put out

To extinguish a fire or flame; to publish or release something; to make an effort.

*He quickly grabbed a fire extinguisher to **put out** the small kitchen fire.*

*The author was excited to **put out** a new book after months of hard work.*

*They decided to **put out** a statement addressing the recent controversy.*

*It requires teamwork to effectively **put out** a complex project on time.*

*She made a conscious effort to **put out** positive vibes and support her friends.*

Move on

To progress or proceed forward; to let go of the past and continue with life.

*After the breakup, she decided it was time to **move on** and focus on herself.*

*They encouraged each other to **move on** from past mistakes and learn from them.*

*It's important to **move on** from negative experiences and embrace a brighter future.*

*He realized it was time to **move on** to new challenges and opportunities in his career.*

*They decided to **move on** as a team and leave behind the setbacks of the previous project.*

Let down

To disappoint or fail someone's expectations; to lower or drop something.

*She felt like she **let down** her team by not meeting the project deadline.*

*It's important to communicate effectively to avoid **letting down** others on the team.*

*He apologized sincerely for **letting down** his friends with his actions.*

*They decided to work together to ensure they wouldn't **let down** their clients.*

*She promised not to **let down** her supporters and worked hard to fulfill her commitments.*

Give away

To donate or provide something for free; to reveal a secret or surprise.

*They decided to **give away** old clothes and toys to a local charity.*

*She chose to **give away** her extra tickets to friends who couldn't afford them.*

*It's important to **give away** knowledge and skills to empower others.*

*He accidentally **gave away** the surprise party by mentioning it to the birthday person.*

*They decided to **give away** free samples to promote the new product.*

Take apart

To disassemble or dismantle; to analyze or understand thoroughly.

*He needed to **take apart** the engine to identify and fix the issue.*

*They decided to **take apart** the old furniture to repurpose the materials.*

*It's crucial to **take apart** complex problems to find effective solutions.*

*She was curious and wanted to **take apart** the electronic device to see how it worked.*

*Before moving, they had to **take apart** the modular furniture for easy transportation.*

Freak out

To react with extreme fear, anxiety, or excitement; to become extremely upset.

*She tends to **freak out** during thunderstorms due to her fear of lightning.*

*He didn't expect her to **freak out** when he*

mentioned the possibility of moving.

*It's important to remain calm and not **freak out** in emergency situations.*

*They were excited and started to **freak out** when they won the lottery.*

*Despite the challenge, he tried not to **freak out** and approach the situation logically.*

Start over

To begin anew; to reset or restart from the beginning.

*After the failure, they decided to **start over** with a fresh approach.*

*He realized the project needed a different direction and chose to **start over**.*

*It's never too late to **start over** and pursue a new career path.*

*They scrapped the initial design and agreed to **start over** with a more innovative concept.*

*She decided to **start over** in a new city to explore different opportunities.*

Crack up

To burst into laughter; to break down mentally or emotionally; to collide or crash.

*The joke made them all **crack up** and laugh uncontrollably.*

*He couldn't help but **crack up** at the amusing situation.*

*They decided to watch a comedy show to **crack up** after a stressful day.*

*She tried to lighten the mood by telling a funny story that made everyone **crack up**.*

*Despite the pressure, he managed not to **crack up** and stay focused on the task.*

Stand by

To be ready or available for assistance or support; to remain loyal or committed.

*They assured him that they would **stand by** him during challenging times.*

In case of an emergency, the rescue team is

*always ready to **stand by**.*

*She promised to **stand by** her friend throughout the difficult decision-making process.*

*Even in the face of adversity, he chose to **stand by** his principles.*

*It's important for friends to **stand by** each other during both good and bad times.*

Put up with

To tolerate or endure; to accept a difficult or unpleasant situation without complaining.

*She has a lot of patience to **put up with** her noisy neighbors.*

*It's challenging to **put up with** constant interruptions while trying to work.*

*He decided he could no longer **put up with** the disrespectful behavior of his colleagues.*

*They chose to **put up with** the inconvenience rather than causing a confrontation.*

*It's admirable how she can **put up with** difficult*

circumstances and remain positive.

Stand around

To remain in a place without any particular purpose;
to loiter or linger.

> *They had to **stand around** and wait for the
> delayed train to arrive.*

> *It's not productive to **stand around** when there's
> work to be done.*

> *People tend to **stand around** chatting near the
> coffee machine during breaks.*

> *While waiting for the event to start, attendees
> began to **stand around** and socialize.*

> *He noticed a group of teenagers who liked to
> **stand around** the park entrance.*

Carry out

To execute or complete a task or action; to implement
or fulfill a plan or project.

*They needed to **carry out** a thorough investigation to understand the cause of the issue.*

*It's crucial to **carry out** safety procedures in case of an emergency.*

*The team worked together to **carry out** the plan and achieve the project goals.*

*He was assigned to **carry out** the experiment and report the results.*

*She had to **carry out** the company's policies and ensure compliance among employees.*

Throw up

To vomit; to expel the contents of the stomach through the mouth.

*After eating something spoiled, she felt the need to **throw up**.*

*He experienced motion sickness during the turbulent flight and had to **throw up**.*

*It's common for children to **throw up** when they have a stomach bug.*

*She couldn't handle the strong smell and had to excuse herself to **throw up**.*

*They advised him to rest and drink water after feeling the urge to **throw up**.*

Pick on

To tease, bully, or harass someone repeatedly; to target or single out for criticism.

*It's important to address and stop anyone who tries to **pick on** others in the workplace.*

*She was determined to help her younger sibling deal with classmates who would **pick on** them.*

*They decided to stand up against the students who liked to **pick on** their friend.*

*He couldn't understand why some people felt the need to **pick on** those who were different.*

*Teachers should be vigilant and intervene when they witness students trying to **pick on** their peers.*

Have over

To invite someone to one's home; to host or entertain guests.

> *They decided to **have over** their friends for a casual dinner gathering.*

> *She enjoys **having over** her relatives during the holidays for a festive celebration.*

> *He often **has over** colleagues for informal meetings and discussions.*

> *They wanted to **have over** new neighbors to welcome them to the community.*

> *Despite their busy schedules, they try to **have over** friends for a movie night regularly.*

Fall apart

To disintegrate or break into pieces; to experience a sudden and complete failure.

> *The old book's pages were so fragile that they started to **fall apart**.*

> *Despite their efforts, the project began to **fall***

apart due to unforeseen challenges.

*She felt like her world was starting to **fall apart** after the unexpected news.*

*The antique furniture started to **fall apart** after years of wear and tear.*

*They had to find a way to prevent the team from **falling apart** during a difficult period.*

Get by

To manage or survive with the available resources; to cope or make do in a challenging situation.

*During tough times, they learned to **get by** with limited financial resources.*

*She found creative ways to **get by** while waiting for a job opportunity.*

*They had to improvise and find ways to **get by** without the usual tools.*

*Despite the setbacks, they managed to **get by** through mutual support and teamwork.*

*He assured his friends that they would **get by***

together despite the challenges they faced.

Break out

To escape or burst out suddenly; to start suddenly, often referring to a negative event or conflict.

*There was chaos when some prisoners tried to **break out** of the jail.*

*The fire alarm went off, prompting everyone to **break out** of the building quickly.*

*They worried that a conflict might **break out** if tensions continued to rise.*

*The news of the virus spreading quickly caused panic to **break out** in the community.*

*Despite their efforts, a disagreement started to **break out** among the team members.*

Wind up

To end up in a particular situation or place; to conclude or finish something.

*Despite their initial disagreements, they managed to **wind up** as close friends.*

*After a series of unexpected events, he found himself **winding up** in a foreign country.*

*They didn't anticipate the journey would **wind up** being so adventurous.*

*Despite the challenges, the project eventually **wound up** being a success.*

*She never thought her career would **wind up** in the field of technology.*

Stick with

To remain loyal or committed to someone or something; to continue with a particular choice or decision.

*Even during tough times, he chose to **stick with** his principles and values.*

*She encouraged her friend to **stick with** the challenging project despite the obstacles.*

*They decided to **stick with** the original plan*

instead of making last-minute changes.

Despite the tempting alternatives, he opted to **stick with** *his current job for the long term.*

It's important to **stick with** *healthy habits for long-term well-being.*

Blow away

To impress or astonish greatly; to cause someone to be extremely impressed or surprised.

The breathtaking scenery **blew away** *all the tourists who visited the national park.*

His performance in the concert **blew away** *both the audience and the critics.*

The new technology **blew away** *everyone in the industry with its innovation.*

They were **blown away** *by the generosity of the community during the fundraising event.*

Her talent and skills in the competition **blew away** *the judges and fellow participants.*

Step aside

To move to the side or out of the way; to withdraw from a position or responsibility.

> *He decided to **step aside** and let the more experienced colleague take the lead.*

> *During the conflict, the leader chose to **step aside** and let the team resolve the issue independently.*

> *She gracefully **stepped aside** to allow the younger generation to take charge.*

> *It's essential for leaders to know when to **step aside** and let others contribute to decision-making.*

> *He was willing to **step aside** and give someone else the opportunity to shine.*

Brush up on

To review or refresh one's knowledge or skills on a particular topic.

> *Before the exam, she decided to **brush up on** her math skills.*

*He took a weekend course to **brush up on** his language proficiency.*

*They spent the summer break to **brush up on** their history knowledge.*

*Before the interview, it's a good idea to **brush up on** the company's background.*

*He realized he needed to **brush up on** his coding skills for the upcoming project.*

Help out

To assist or provide aid; to contribute support or assistance.

*She always volunteers to **help out** at community events and projects.*

*He offered to **help out** with the heavy lifting during the relocation.*

*They decided to **help out** their neighbors by mowing the lawn while they were away.*

*During the crisis, various organizations came together to **help out** affected communities.*

*He was more than willing to **help out** his colleagues with their workload.*

Rip off

To charge too much for something; to copy or imitate closely, often with negative connotations.

*He felt that the prices at the fancy restaurant were a **rip off** for the portion sizes.*

*She warned her friends not to buy from the street vendor, as they might **rip them off**.*

*They discovered that the designer bags they bought were **rip-offs** of the original brand.*

*Consumers should be cautious of online sellers who may try to **rip them off** with counterfeit products.*

*He was disappointed to find out that the repair service was a **rip off** with hidden fees.*

Turn on

To switch on or activate a device; to become

interested or excited about something.

> *She reached over to **turn on** the lamp and illuminate the room.*

> *He decided to **turn on** the TV to catch up on the latest news.*

> *They wanted to **turn on** the heating system to warm up the house.*

> *After attending the concert, she started to **turn on** to the music genre.*

> *Learning about space exploration made him **turn on** to science and astronomy.*

Stand down

To resign or withdraw from a position or responsibility; to cease action or resistance.

> *After years of service, the leader decided to **stand down** and let a new person take charge.*

> *They urged the protesters to **stand down** and engage in peaceful dialogue.*

> *It was a relief for him to finally **stand down** from*

his demanding role.

*She felt it was time to **stand down** from the committee and focus on personal priorities.*

*Despite initial disagreements, both parties agreed to **stand down** and find common ground.*

Cut out

To remove or eliminate; to cease or stop doing something; to leave abruptly.

*They decided to **cut out** unhealthy snacks from their diet for better nutrition.*

*After realizing the negative impact, he chose to **cut out** excessive screen time.*

*It was time for her to **cut out** negative influences and focus on personal growth.*

*He needed to **cut out** unnecessary expenses to save money for future goals.*

*Feeling unfulfilled, she decided to **cut out** from her current job and explore new opportunities.*

Hit on

To flirt with or attempt to romantically attract
someone; to make advances or show interest.

*He decided to **hit on** the person he found
interesting at the party.*

*Despite being shy, she mustered the courage to
hit on her crush.*

*They laughed about the awkward ways people try
to **hit on** each other in social settings.*

*It's essential to approach respectfully when trying
to **hit on** someone you're interested in.*

*He didn't want to come across as too forward
when attempting to **hit on** the new colleague.*

Go on

To continue or proceed; to take place; to express
disbelief or surprise.

*Despite the challenges, they decided to **go on**
with the project.*

*She listened intently as the speaker began to **go***

on about the latest developments.

*As the day **went on**, they encountered unexpected obstacles.*

*He couldn't believe it when the improbable story started to **go on**.*

*They decided to **go on** with the plan despite the initial doubts.*

Come through

To fulfill a promise or commitment; to successfully overcome a challenge or difficulty.

*She always **comes through** when her friends need support.*

*Despite the setbacks, they managed to **come through** and achieve their goals.*

*He assured his team that they would **come through** the challenging period.*

*Even in tough times, they found a way to **come through** with innovative solutions.*

*She was grateful that her family **came through***

Take up

To start or begin a hobby, activity, or occupation; to occupy space or time.

*He decided to **take up** painting as a form of creative expression.*

*She wanted to **take up** a new sport to stay active and healthy.*

*They encouraged him to **take up** a musical instrument for personal enjoyment.*

*She found it fulfilling to **take up** gardening as a relaxing hobby.*

*Despite a busy schedule, he managed to **take up** a part-time course for self-improvement.*

Strike out

To fail or be unsuccessful; to be unable to achieve a goal or succeed in an endeavor.

*Despite multiple attempts, he continued to **strike out** in finding a suitable job.*

*She felt disappointed when her idea **struck out** during the pitch meeting.*

*They realized they needed to revise the strategy after repeatedly **striking out**.*

*He acknowledged that not every idea would succeed and was prepared for some to **strike out**.*

*Despite putting in the effort, they were unfortunate and **struck out** in securing the sponsorship.*

Tear down

To demolish or dismantle a structure; to criticize severely or disapprove strongly.

*They decided to **tear down** the old building and construct a modern one in its place.*

*Despite its historical significance, the city council chose to **tear down** the aging monument.*

*He felt the need to **tear down** the outdated*

policies that hindered progress.

*During the renovation, they had to **tear down** the walls to create an open space.*

*It's important to provide constructive feedback rather than **tear down** someone's efforts.*

Get away

To escape or leave a place, especially quickly; to take a break or go on vacation.

*She needed to **get away** from the stress of work and relax for a few days.*

*They decided to **get away** to the countryside to enjoy nature and fresh air.*

*He felt the need to **get away** from the city's hustle and bustle for a peaceful retreat.*

*Despite the busy schedule, they planned a weekend trip to **get away** from routine.*

*After the challenging project, the team decided to **get away** for a team-building retreat.*

Put off

To delay or postpone; to discourage or make someone lose interest.

*They had to **put off** the meeting until everyone could attend.*

*Despite the initial excitement, unexpected issues forced them to **put off** the event.*

*He didn't want to **put off** making important decisions any longer.*

*The bad weather forced them to **put off** the outdoor event to a later date.*

*They realized the negative impact of continuously **putting off** important tasks.*

Move over

To change position to make room for someone else; to yield or give space.

*He politely asked the person next to him to **move over** so that others could sit.*

Despite the crowded bus, people were willing to

__move over__ to accommodate more passengers.

She gestured for the group to __move over__ and make space for the newcomers.

During the event, they had to __move over__ to create an aisle for emergency access.

He kindly asked his friend to __move over__ on the bench so that there was enough space for both.

Give out

To distribute or hand out; to stop working or fail; to run out of a particular resource.

They decided to __give out__ pamphlets to raise awareness about the cause.

The old printer finally __gave out__ after years of reliable service.

During the charity event, they __gave out__ free meals to those in need.

As the batteries __gave out__, they quickly replaced them to keep the device running.

They had to improvise after realizing they had

__given out__ all the promotional materials.

Break down

To stop functioning; to analyze or examine in detail; to collapse emotionally.

The car __broke down__ on the highway, and they had to call for assistance.

She decided to __break down__ the complex problem into smaller, manageable tasks.

He couldn't help but __break down__ in tears after receiving the heartbreaking news.

During the workshop, they took time to __break down__ the steps of the process for better understanding.

Despite the pressure, he didn't __break down__ and continued working towards his goal.

Make out

To perceive or understand something; to engage in romantic or sexual activity.

*It was difficult to **make out** the details in the dimly lit room.*

*Despite the language barrier, they managed to **make out** the main points of the conversation.*

*They decided to **make out** in the park, enjoying the romantic atmosphere.*

*It was challenging to **make out** what the distant figure was doing.*

*She tried to **make out** the handwriting on the old letter.*

Give up

To surrender or stop trying; to relinquish or abandon a pursuit or goal.

*Despite the challenges, they refused to **give up** on their dreams.*

*He decided to **give up** smoking for the sake of his health.*

*After numerous attempts, she felt it was time to **give up** on the unattainable goal.*

*They encouraged him not to **give up** in the face of adversity.*

*She was determined not to **give up** even when the situation seemed hopeless.*

Think over

To consider or reflect on something carefully before making a decision.

*Before accepting the job offer, she needed time to **think over** the terms and conditions.*

*They advised him to **think over** the implications before committing to the agreement.*

*It's important to **think over** major decisions to avoid regrets later.*

*She took a weekend to **think over** her options regarding the career change.*

*He asked for some time to **think over** the proposal before providing a response.*

Bag on

To criticize or mock someone; to express disapproval
or make fun of.

*It's not fair to **bag on** someone for their choices
without understanding their perspective.*

*Despite the challenges, she chose not to **bag on**
her teammate for the mistake.*

*He felt hurt when others started to **bag on** his
creative project.*

*They decided to support each other rather than
bagging on each other's weaknesses.*

*Constructive feedback is essential, but it's not
helpful to constantly **bag on** someone.*

Get away with

To escape punishment or consequences for an action;
to succeed in doing something without being caught.

*He thought he could **get away with** skipping the
assignment, but the teacher noticed.*

*Despite the risky behavior, they managed to **get***

away with their adventurous escapade.

*It's not advisable to attempt to **get away with** unethical practices in the workplace.*

*She wondered if he would **get away with** breaking the rules once again.*

*They were surprised to see someone **getting away with** shoplifting in broad daylight.*

Look after

To take care of or watch over someone; to be responsible for their well-being.

*She promised to **look after** her friend's pets while they were away on vacation.*

*He was grateful for the neighbors who offered to **look after** his plants during his absence.*

*Despite the busy schedule, they made sure to **look after** their younger siblings.*

*It's essential to have someone reliable to **look after** your children when you're not around.*

*She volunteered to **look after** the elderly*

members of the community during the winter season.

Sneak around

To move quietly and stealthily; to engage in secretive or furtive behavior.

*They decided to **sneak around** the house to avoid waking up the sleeping baby.*

*Despite the prohibition, some students attempted to **sneak around** during the night.*

*She noticed someone trying to **sneak around** the office after hours.*

*It's not advisable to **sneak around** in restricted areas without proper authorization.*

*They were caught trying to **sneak around** and take a shortcut through the restricted zone.*

Speak up

To express one's opinion or thoughts openly and confidently; to talk louder.

*It's important to **speak up** when you witness injustice or wrongdoing.*

*Despite her initial hesitation, she found the courage to **speak up** during the meeting.*

*He encouraged the shy students to **speak up** and share their perspectives in class.*

*During the discussion, everyone was encouraged to **speak up** and contribute their ideas.*

*She had to **speak up** as the noise in the room made it difficult to hear.*

Put on

To wear clothing or accessories; to apply makeup or a performance; to assume a certain demeanor.

*She decided to **put on** a warm coat before heading out into the cold weather.*

*He was excited to **put on** the costume for the school play.*

*They needed to **put on** their game faces and focus on the upcoming competition.*

*Before the party, she took time to **put on** her favorite makeup and style her hair.*

*He chose to **put on** a brave front despite the challenging situation.*

Go out

To leave one's residence; to engage in social activities or a romantic relationship.

*They decided to **go out** for dinner to celebrate the special occasion.*

*Despite the rain, they still wanted to **go out** and enjoy the evening.*

*He asked her if she would like to **go out** for coffee sometime.*

*She enjoys the weekends when she can **go out** and explore the city.*

*They usually **go out** with friends on Friday nights for some entertainment.*

Go by

To pass or elapse; to be known by a certain name or title.

> Time tends to **go by** quickly when you're having fun.

> She watched the seasons **go by** as the trees changed colors.

> They knew him by the nickname that had **gone by** for years.

> As the train **went by**, they waved to the passengers inside.

> He remembered the days that **went by** when they used to play in the park.

Blow up

To explode or burst; to become extremely angry; to inflate or enlarge.

> The scientists observed the controlled explosion as they made the building **blow up**.

> He tends to **blow up** when things don't go as

planned.

*She decided to **blow up** balloons for the birthday party decoration.*

*It's not healthy to **blow up** over minor inconveniences.*

*They witnessed the fireworks **blow up** in a spectacular display.*

Straighten out

To resolve or clarify a situation; to improve or correct something.

*They needed a meeting to **straighten out** the misunderstanding between team members.*

*It took some time, but they managed to **straighten out** the confusion in the project plan.*

*She decided to **straighten out** her priorities and focus on what truly mattered.*

*He asked for professional advice to help him **straighten out** his financial troubles.*

It's essential to communicate openly to

***straighten out** any relationship issues.*

Come from

To originate or have a source; to be born or raised in a particular place.

*The family recipe **comes from** her grandmother, who was an excellent cook.*

*He proudly stated that he **comes from** a long line of skilled artisans.*

*The tradition of storytelling **comes from** their cultural heritage.*

*She mentioned that her unique perspective **comes from** her diverse upbringing.*

*The inspiration for the artwork **comes from** the artist's experiences and emotions.*

Put away

To store or place an item in its designated location; to save or set aside for later.

*After cooking, she made sure to **put away** the ingredients and clean the kitchen.*

*He decided to **put away** some money every month for future expenses.*

*It's important to **put away** your belongings neatly to maintain an organized living space.*

*She asked the children to **put away** their toys after playing in the living room.*

*They decided to **put away** the winter clothes as spring approached.*

Unit 3

Hold on

To wait or pause; to grasp or cling to something for support.

*He asked her to **hold on** for a moment while he fetched the documents.*

*They needed to **hold on** until the storm passed before continuing the outdoor event.*

*She tightly **held on** to the railing as she descended the steep staircase.*

*He requested everyone to **hold on** while technical issues with the presentation were resolved.*

*It's crucial to **hold on** to your values even in challenging situations.*

Knock down

To demolish or destroy a structure; to bring someone to the ground by force.

*They decided to **knock down** the old building and construct a modern one.*

*He accidentally **knocked down** the tower of building blocks his sibling was building.*

*The strong winds threatened to **knock down** the fragile tents at the campsite.*

*She practiced martial arts to learn how to **knock down** opponents in self-defense.*

*The wrecking ball was used to **knock down** the walls of the abandoned factory.*

Walk around

To move about on foot; to explore an area or space by walking.

> They decided to **walk around** the neighborhood to enjoy the fresh air.

> She likes to **walk around** the park and admire the beauty of nature.

> He suggested they **walk around** the city and discover hidden gems.

> Despite the busy schedule, they took a break to **walk around** the office building.

> It's therapeutic to **walk around** and clear your mind when feeling stressed.

Weird out

To make someone feel uncomfortable or strange; to cause a sense of unease or confusion.

> The surreal artwork tended to **weird out** those who viewed it for the first time.

> He intentionally told bizarre stories to **weird out**

his friends during the camping trip.

They played eerie music to **weird out** the guests at the Halloween party.

It's not polite to deliberately **weird out** someone who is unfamiliar with your sense of humor.

The unexpected turn of events managed to **weird out** the entire audience.

Break up

To end a relationship; to disintegrate into smaller parts.

After years of disagreements, they decided to **break up** and go their separate ways.

The company had to **break up** into smaller divisions to adapt to market changes.

Despite their efforts, the fight caused the group to **break up** and disband.

She felt the need to **break up** with her old habits and start afresh.

They realized it was time to **break up** the large

project into more manageable tasks.

Pull off

To successfully accomplish a challenging task; to execute a plan effectively.

> *Against all odds, they managed to **pull off** a spectacular performance.*

> *He had to use his creativity to **pull off** the last-minute project successfully.*

> *Despite the complications, they were able to **pull off** the event without any major issues.*

> *It seemed impossible at first, but they were determined to **pull off** the daring heist.*

> *She needed to carefully plan to **pull off** the surprise birthday party.*

Buckle up

To fasten one's seatbelt; to prepare for a challenging situation.

*Before the car started moving, they reminded everyone to **buckle up**.*

*As the plane prepared for takeoff, the flight attendant instructed passengers to **buckle up**.*

*She always makes sure to **buckle up** before driving, prioritizing safety.*

*They were told to **buckle up** for a turbulent ride through the stormy weather.*

*It's crucial to **buckle up** mentally when facing challenges in the professional world.*

Dish out

To serve food; to distribute or dispense something, usually criticism or punishment.

*She skillfully **dished out** a delicious three-course meal for the guests.*

*The coach wasn't afraid to **dish out** constructive criticism to improve performance.*

*During the charity event, they decided to **dish out** meals to those in need.*

*He felt it was time to **dish out** consequences for those who broke the rules.*

*It's important to be fair when **dishing out** responsibilities among team members.*

Stick up for

To defend or support someone; to take someone's side in an argument or disagreement.

*She always **sticks up for** her friends when they face unjust criticism.*

*He decided to **stick up for** the underdog in the heated debate.*

*It's important to **stick up for** your values even when facing opposition.*

*They were grateful that someone **stuck up for** them during the challenging situation.*

*She chose to **stick up for** her principles, even if it meant going against the majority.*

Turn in

To submit or hand in; to go to bed or retire for the night.

*They were given a deadline to **turn in** their assignments by the end of the week.*

*After a long day at work, he decided to **turn in** early and get some rest.*

*She realized she forgot to **turn in** the application form and rushed to submit it on time.*

*They were relieved to **turn in** the project after weeks of hard work.*

*It's important to **turn in** valuable items to the lost and found department.*

Drop by

To visit someone casually and without prior notice.

*She decided to **drop by** her friend's house to say hello and catch up.*

*He often **dropped by** the local cafe for a quick coffee during his lunch break.*

*They appreciated it when friends **dropped by** to share good news or offer support.*

*She promised to **drop by** the office later to discuss the upcoming project.*

*It's always a pleasant surprise when unexpected guests **drop by** for a visit.*

Slip away

To leave quietly or unnoticed; to escape or disappear subtly.

*He decided to **slip away** from the party without saying goodbye to avoid attention.*

*They managed to **slip away** from the crowded event and enjoy some private time.*

*She tried to **slip away** from the meeting early to attend another appointment.*

*Despite the chaos, the cat was able to **slip away** and explore the neighborhood.*

*They decided to **slip away** from the bustling city for a quiet weekend retreat.*

Wash up

To clean oneself, typically by washing hands and face;
to clean dishes or utensils.

*After playing outdoors, the children were
reminded to **wash up** before dinner.*

*He always made sure to **wash up** thoroughly
after working in the garden.*

*She decided to **wash up** the dishes immediately
after finishing the meal.*

*They were taught the importance of **washing up**
before handling food in the kitchen.*

*Before the guests arrived, she excused herself to
wash up and freshen up.*

Lash out

To express strong anger or frustration, often by
attacking verbally or physically.

*Feeling overwhelmed, he unintentionally **lashed
out** at his colleagues during the meeting.*

*She tends to **lash out** when under stress, but later*

regrets her harsh words.

*They advised him to find healthier ways to cope with stress instead of **lashing out**.*

*It's important to address the underlying issues rather than **lashing out** at others.*

*He decided to take a break and calm down before **lashing out** in anger.*

Sink in

To be fully understood or realized; to become emotionally comprehended.

*It took some time for the news to **sink in** after they heard about the unexpected loss.*

*As she reflected on the achievement, the significance began to **sink in**.*

*It's often challenging for major life changes to immediately **sink in** and feel real.*

*He stared at the winning lottery ticket, waiting for the reality to **sink in**.*

It can take a while for the consequences of a

*decision to **sink in**.*

Play along

To pretend to agree or cooperate with something for amusement or to avoid conflict.

*She decided to **play along** with the prank, pretending to be surprised.*

*During the improvisational game, they were encouraged to **play along** with any scenario.*

*He chose to **play along** with the joke, maintaining a lighthearted atmosphere.*

*It's important to know when to **play along** with humor, even in serious situations.*

*They all agreed to **play along** with the surprise party plans to keep it a secret.*

Get ahead

To make progress or succeed, especially in a competitive or career context.

*By consistently working hard, she managed to **get ahead** in her career.*

*They believed that education was the key to helping them **get ahead** in life.*

*He sought opportunities to learn and grow professionally to **get ahead** in the industry.*

*It's essential to set goals and strive to **get ahead** rather than staying stagnant.*

*Despite challenges, he remained determined to **get ahead** and achieve his dreams.*

Run out

To exhaust the supply of something; to leave a place quickly.

*They realized they had **run out** of milk and needed to buy more from the store.*

*It's frustrating to discover you've **run out** of a crucial ingredient while cooking.*

*He had to make a quick trip to the gas station because his car had **run out** of fuel.*

*They decided to **run out** of the building when the fire alarm sounded.*

*She panicked when she saw the warning that the printer was about to **run out** of ink.*

Hop in

To enter a vehicle or jump into a place quickly.

*As they approached the car, she gestured for everyone to **hop in**.*

*He decided to **hop in** a cab rather than waiting for the bus in the rain.*

*They invited their friends to **hop in** the car for an impromptu road trip.*

*She told the kids to **hop in** the backseat as they prepared for a family outing.*

*Despite the rush, they managed to **hop in** the elevator before the doors closed.*

Cut back

To reduce or decrease; to consume less of something.

> *They decided to **cut back** on expenses to save money for a future vacation.*

> *She realized it was necessary to **cut back** on sugary snacks for better health.*

> *He committed to **cutting back** on screen time to improve productivity.*

> *They decided to **cut back** on unnecessary meetings to use time more efficiently.*

> *It's beneficial to **cut back** on energy consumption for a more sustainable lifestyle.*

Think through

To consider thoroughly; to carefully plan or evaluate a situation.

> *Before making a decision, it's essential to **think through** all the possible outcomes.*

> *She encouraged her team to **think through** the project details before implementation.*

> *They took the time to **think through** the

implications of their business strategy.

*He always tries to **think through** the consequences before taking action.*

*It's crucial to **think through** a major life change before making a commitment.*

Pop out

To quickly appear or become visible; to exit briefly.

*They watched in amazement as the magician made a coin **pop out** from behind his ear.*

*She decided to **pop out** of the meeting briefly to grab a cup of coffee.*

*He asked her to **pop out** of the room so he could plan a surprise for her.*

*During the presentation, a surprising statistic made everyone's eyes **pop out**.*

*They were startled when they saw a colorful bird suddenly **pop out** from the bushes.*

Beat up

To physically harm or assault someone; to defeat or
surpass in a competition.

> *He was unfairly **beaten up** by a group of bullies
> on his way home.*

> *Despite the odds, they managed to **beat up** their
> opponents in the final match.*

> *She witnessed a superhero in the comic book
> **beating up** the villains.*

> *It's important to stand up against injustice and
> not let others **beat up** on the weak.*

> *They were determined to **beat up** the challenge
> and emerge victorious.*

Take away

To remove or carry something from one place to
another; to eliminate or subtract.

> *He asked the waiter to **take away** the empty
> plates after finishing the meal.*

> *They decided to **take away** the distractions in the*

workspace for better focus.

*She wanted to **take away** a valuable lesson from the challenging experience.*

*It's important to **take away** unnecessary stressors from daily life for better well-being.*

*They agreed to **take away** some key points from the meeting to implement in their projects.*

Kick out

To dismiss or expel someone from a place or group.

*After repeated violations, they had no choice but to **kick out** the disruptive student.*

*The manager decided to **kick out** the employee who consistently violated company policies.*

*They had to **kick out** the unruly guest from the party for causing trouble.*

*It's important to maintain a respectful environment and be prepared to **kick out** troublemakers.*

He was warned several times before they finally

*had to **kick him out** of the club.*

Blend in

To become or appear similar or inconspicuous within a particular environment.

*She tried to **blend in** with the crowd by wearing casual clothing.*

*When traveling to a foreign country, it's helpful to **blend in** with the local customs.*

*He had to find a way to **blend in** at the costume party without standing out too much.*

*They recommended using earthy tones to **blend in** with the natural surroundings during the hike.*

*To avoid being noticed, she attempted to **blend in** with the background.*

Head up

To be in charge of; to lead or manage a team or project.

*She was promoted to **head up** the marketing department due to her expertise.*

*He volunteered to **head up** the charity event and coordinate the volunteers.*

*They appointed a seasoned executive to **head up** the new division of the company.*

*She had the experience and skills needed to successfully **head up** the research team.*

*He was honored to be chosen to **head up** the community project for positive change.*

Blurt out

To unintentionally say something impulsively or without thinking.

*She accidentally **blurted out** the surprise party plans in front of the birthday person.*

*He tends to **blurt out** his opinions without considering the consequences.*

*Despite the effort to keep it a secret, she **blurted out** the confidential information.*

*It's important to think before speaking to avoid **blurting out** sensitive information.*

*Feeling nervous, he **blurted out** the answer to the question without hesitation.*

Rely on

To depend on or trust someone or something for support or assistance.

*During challenging times, you can always **rely on** your friends for emotional support.*

*She knew she could **rely on** her team to meet the project deadline successfully.*

*It's essential to **rely on** accurate information when making important decisions.*

*He decided to **rely on** his experience and expertise to overcome the obstacles.*

*When facing difficulties, it's important to **rely on** your inner strength and resilience.*

Suck up to

To overly flatter or seek favor from someone, often in a insincere way.

*He constantly tries to **suck up to** the boss in hopes of getting a promotion.*

*She noticed her colleague was attempting to **suck up to** the supervisor during the meeting.*

*It's not genuine when people **suck up to** others just to gain personal benefits.*

*He decided to focus on his work rather than **sucking up to** higher-ups for recognition.*

*She was unimpressed by the attempts of some team members to **suck up to** the team leader.*

Reason with

To engage in a discussion or argument in an attempt to persuade or convince.

*She tried to **reason with** her friend to find a compromise in their disagreement.*

*It's important to **reason with** others and find*

common ground in conflicts.

*He attempted to **reason with** his parents to allow him more freedom.*

*They decided to **reason with** the opposing party to avoid unnecessary confrontations.*

*It's challenging to **reason with** someone who is unwilling to listen to different perspectives.*

Show off

To display or boast about one's abilities, possessions, or achievements in a proud or ostentatious manner.

*She couldn't resist the opportunity to **show off** her impressive art collection to guests.*

*He tends to **show off** his new gadgets whenever he gets the chance.*

*They decided not to **show off** their wealth and instead focused on philanthropy.*

*It's important to share accomplishments without coming across as trying to **show off**.*

During the competition, each participant had the

*chance to **show off** their unique talents.*

Back up

To support or defend someone in a dispute or challenging situation.

*She promised to **back him up** during the argument with their colleague.*

*It's crucial to have friends who will **back you up** in times of need.*

*They decided to **back up** their teammate when facing criticism from the coach.*

*He appreciated that his family always **backed him up** in pursuing his dreams.*

*It's important to **back up** your colleagues when they face unjust accusations.*

Go along with

To agree or comply with someone's suggestion, plan, or idea.

*She decided to **go along with** the team's decision, even though she had reservations.*

*He was willing to **go along with** the proposed changes to improve efficiency.*

*They agreed to **go along with** the group's plan for the upcoming project.*

*It's important to have team members who are willing to **go along with** the majority's decision.*

*She chose to **go along with** the new policy rather than resist the change.*

Max out

To reach the maximum limit or capacity; to use or consume something to the fullest extent.

*He decided to **max out** his credit card during the holiday shopping spree.*

*After intense training, she managed to **max out** her physical endurance.*

*They planned to **max out** the venue's capacity for the concert.*

*It's important not to **max out** your energy early in the day for better productivity.*

*He aimed to **max out** his potential in every aspect of his life.*

Buy into

To believe or accept an idea, concept, or philosophy, especially when influenced or persuaded.

*She was hesitant at first, but eventually, she decided to **buy into** the new business proposal.*

*They encouraged the team to **buy into** the company's vision for future success.*

*He was skeptical at first but started to **buy into** the benefits of the new technology.*

*It's essential for employees to **buy into** the company culture for a harmonious work environment.*

*They worked hard to get everyone to **buy into** the idea of a more sustainable lifestyle.*

Slip up

To make a mistake or error, often unintentionally; to fail to maintain control or composure.

*During the presentation, he accidentally **slipped up** and revealed confidential information.*

*It's common to **slip up** when learning a new skill, but practice helps improve performance.*

*She apologized after realizing she had **slipped up** and given the wrong directions.*

*It's important to acknowledge and learn from the moments when you **slip up** in life.*

*He tried not to **slip up** during the high-pressure situation, but the stress got to him.*

Get back at

To seek revenge or retaliate against someone for a perceived wrongdoing.

*After the argument, he decided to **get back at** his friend by playing a prank.*

She didn't appreciate the betrayal and planned to

get back at the person responsible.

They plotted to get back at the rival team for their previous defeat.

Instead of resorting to revenge, she chose to forgive rather than get back at her colleague.

He warned against trying to get back at others, emphasizing the importance of forgiveness.

Kick in

To contribute or provide financial support; to come into effect or start working.

He decided to kick in some extra money to help cover the cost of the party.

They asked everyone to kick in a small amount for the charity fundraiser.

After weeks of training, the benefits of the exercise routine began to kick in.

The medicine took some time to kick in, providing relief from the pain.

It's important for team members to kick in their

efforts for the success of the project.

Burn out

To experience physical or emotional exhaustion due to prolonged stress or overwork.

*She had been working long hours, and it was evident that she was starting to **burn out**.*

*They emphasized the importance of taking breaks to avoid **burning out** in the demanding job.*

*He realized he needed to make lifestyle changes to prevent **burning out** from constant pressure.*

*It's crucial to recognize the signs of **burnout** and take proactive steps to address it.*

*After a period of intense stress, she decided to take a vacation to prevent **burning out**.*

Put up to

To influence or encourage someone to do something, often mischievous or risky.

Lay off

To terminate or dismiss employees from their jobs, often due to economic reasons.

*The company had to **lay off** several employees during the economic downturn.*

*He was devastated when he heard the news that the company would **lay off** a significant portion of the workforce.*

*They had to make the difficult decision to **lay off** workers to sustain the business.*

*During tough times, companies may need to **lay off** employees to stay afloat.*

*She empathized with her colleagues who were affected by the decision to **lay off** staff.*

Break in

To enter a place forcibly or illegally, especially with

criminal intent.

> *They were alarmed when they discovered signs of someone attempting to **break in** to their home.*

> *He called the police after witnessing a suspicious person trying to **break in** to a neighbor's car.*

> *It's important to secure windows and doors to prevent burglars from attempting to **break in**.*

> *They upgraded their home security system after a recent **break-in** in the neighborhood.*

> *The alarm system was activated when someone tried to **break in** during the night.*

Rat out

To inform on or betray someone, especially to authorities or others in a group.

> *He decided to **rat out** his accomplice in exchange for a reduced sentence.*

> *She felt guilty after **ratting out** her friend to the teacher about the mischievous prank.*

> *They promised not to **rat out** each other, even*

*It's essential to maintain trust among friends and avoid **ratting out** others for personal gain.*

*He regretted the decision to **rat out** his colleagues, realizing the consequences of betrayal.*

Shake up

To cause a significant change or disruption; to shock or disturb someone or something.

*The unexpected announcement about layoffs **shook up** the entire company.*

*They decided to **shake up** the traditional approach and introduce innovative ideas.*

*The earthquake **shook up** the residents, causing them to reevaluate their preparedness.*

Act out

To behave badly, especially when unhappy or stressed; to perform a role or character in an exaggerated manner.

*Children may **act out** when they are unable to articulate their frustrations verbally.*

*She tends to **act out** her favorite scenes from movies during playtime.*

*It's important to find healthy ways to cope with stress instead of **acting out** negatively.*

*He decided to **act out** a scene from the play to demonstrate his acting skills.*

*Teens may **act out** as a way to seek attention or deal with internal conflicts.*

Settle in

To become comfortable or established in a new place or situation.

*It took a few weeks for the new employees to **settle in** and feel part of the team.*

*After moving to a new city, it took some time for her family to **settle in** and adapt.*

*They decided to take a break and let the dust settle before trying to **settle in** again.*

*It's important to give yourself time to **settle in** when faced with a major life change.*

*The students began to **settle in** and focus on their studies after the initial adjustment period.*

Go ahead

To proceed or start without hesitation; to give permission to do something.

*He encouraged them to **go ahead** with the project, confident in their abilities.*

*After receiving the green light, they were ready to **go ahead** and implement the plan.*

*She hesitated but eventually decided to **go ahead** and book the flight for her dream vacation.*

*Despite the challenges, they were determined to **go ahead** and organize the event.*

*The teacher gave them the nod to **go ahead** with their creative ideas for the class project.*

Butter up

To flatter or praise someone excessively, often with
the intention of gaining favor or influence.

*She decided to **butter up** her boss before asking
for a raise.*

*He attempted to **butter up** the committee
members with compliments before presenting his
proposal.*

*It's important to be genuine rather than
buttering up others for personal gain.*

*They noticed the attempt to **butter up** the judge
with compliments during the competition.*

*He preferred honest feedback rather than having
people constantly **butter him up**.*

Come off

To be perceived or received in a particular way; to
succeed or fail in a specific manner.

*The speech **came off** well, leaving a positive
impression on the audience.*

*The joke didn't **come off** as intended, leading to an awkward silence.*

*They were relieved that the event **came off** smoothly despite initial concerns.*

*Her plan to surprise him with a gift **came off** perfectly, and he was genuinely touched.*

*It's important to consider how your actions will **come off** to others in different situations.*

Pop in

To visit someone briefly and informally; to appear or happen unexpectedly.

*She decided to **pop in** and surprise her friend on the way home.*

*They appreciated when friends **popped in** to check on them during challenging times.*

*He didn't expect her to **pop in** during his work hours, but he welcomed the visit.*

*It's a good idea to **pop in** and say hello to neighbors every once in a while.*

*They were caught off guard when the idea suddenly **popped in** during the brainstorming session.*

Stay away

To keep a distance; to avoid or refrain from going to a particular place or person.

*After catching a cold, he decided to **stay away** from the office to avoid spreading germs.*

*They were advised to **stay away** from the construction site for safety reasons.*

*She chose to **stay away** from negative influences and focus on her personal growth.*

*It's crucial to **stay away** from risky behaviors that could harm your well-being.*

*He decided to **stay away** from social media for a while to clear his mind.*

Go down

To happen or unfold, often in a specific way; to

decrease in value or quality.

> They were excited to see how the new policy would **go down** with the employees.

> The event **went down** in history as a memorable and successful celebration.

> She wondered how the news would **go down** with the public and prepared for various reactions.

> It's important to consider how your actions will **go down** with those around you.

> Despite initial concerns, the changes **went down** well with the majority of the team.

Chip in

To contribute or donate a small amount of money or effort towards a common goal.

> Everyone decided to **chip in** for a colleague's farewell gift.

> He was grateful when friends offered to **chip in** and help with the moving process.

> They encouraged each team member to **chip in**

ideas for the upcoming project.

*It's essential for everyone to **chip in** and collaborate for the success of the group.*

*They decided to **chip in** their time and skills to support a local community initiative.*

Step out

To leave a place briefly, often for a short period of time.

*She needed to **step out** of the meeting to take an important phone call.*

*He decided to **step out** for some fresh air after working for several hours.*

*They planned to **step out** of the office for a quick lunch break.*

*It's common to **step out** of the room during a long conference to stretch your legs.*

*She asked if they could **step out** of the party for a moment to have a private conversation.*

Step up

To take on more responsibility or a more prominent role; to increase effort or performance.

*He was ready to **step up** and lead the team in the absence of the manager.*

*They encouraged everyone to **step up** their efforts to meet the project deadline.*

*She decided to **step up** her involvement in the community by volunteering for various activities.*

*It's essential for team members to **step up** and support each other during challenging times.*

*The coach challenged the players to **step up** their performance in the crucial match.*

Cool off

To become less angry, agitated, or heated; to relax or calm down.

*After the argument, they needed some time to **cool off** before discussing the issue.*

*She decided to take a walk to **cool off** and clear*

her mind after a stressful day.

*It's advisable to **cool off** before responding to a provoking email or message.*

*He suggested a break to **cool off** the tension in the meeting room.*

*They chose to **cool off** by spending a relaxing weekend in nature.*

Put in

To invest time, effort, or work into a task or activity.

*He decided to **put in** extra hours to meet the project deadline.*

*She was determined to **put in** the effort needed to excel in her studies.*

*They encouraged employees to **put in** innovative ideas for process improvement.*

*It's important to **put in** consistent effort to achieve long-term goals.*

*He was recognized for consistently **putting in** hard work and dedication to his job.*

Seek out

To actively look for or search for something or
someone.

> *He decided to **seek out** new opportunities after
> completing his degree.*
>
> *They actively **sought out** feedback to improve
> their performance.*
>
> *She decided to **seek out** a mentor to guide her in
> her career.*
>
> *It's essential to **seek out** diverse perspectives for a
> well-rounded understanding of a topic.*
>
> *They encouraged employees to **seek out**
> professional development opportunities.*

Bail on

To cancel plans or abandon someone or something
unexpectedly.

> *He decided to **bail on** the party at the last minute
> due to an emergency.*
>
> *She felt disappointed when her friend chose to*

***bail on** their weekend getaway.*

*They were frustrated when the team member decided to **bail on** the important presentation.*

*It's important to communicate if you need to **bail on** a commitment to avoid misunderstandings.*

*He apologized for having to **bail on** the dinner plans due to unexpected work commitments.*

Bring down

To reduce or lower something, such as a price, a person's mood, or a level of difficulty.

*They decided to **bring down** the cost of the product to make it more affordable.*

*She tried to **bring down** the tension in the room with a light-hearted joke.*

*The coach aimed to **bring down** the stress levels of the team before the important match.*

*It's important to find ways to **bring down** stress and promote mental well-being.*

*He successfully **brought down** the difficulty level*

of the task with his innovative approach.

Set up

To arrange or prepare something, such as a meeting, an event, or equipment.

> *She volunteered to **set up** the conference room for the important presentation.*

> *They needed time to **set up** the stage and sound system for the concert.*

> *He took responsibility to **set up** the meeting with key stakeholders.*

> *It's crucial to **set up** the equipment properly for a successful live broadcast.*

> *They collaborated to **set up** the charity event to raise funds for a noble cause.*

Cheat on

To be unfaithful to a romantic partner by engaging in a romantic or sexual relationship with someone else.

*He deeply regretted his decision to **cheat on** his girlfriend and sought forgiveness.*

*She discovered that her partner had been **cheating on** her for months, leading to a breakup.*

*They decided to end the relationship after realizing that one of them had been **cheating on** the other.*

*It's important to communicate openly to address issues rather than resorting to **cheating on** a partner.*

*She felt betrayed when she found out that her husband had been **cheating on** her.*

Live up to

To meet or fulfill the expectations, standards, or ideals set by oneself or others.

*He worked hard to **live up to** the high expectations set by his parents.*

*She strives to **live up to** the values and principles she believes in.*

*They felt a sense of responsibility to **live up to** the trust placed in them by their colleagues.*

*It's essential to set realistic goals and work consistently to **live up to** them.*

*She was determined to **live up to** the legacy of her successful predecessors in the field.*

Bounce back

To recover quickly from a setback or difficult situation.

*After facing a failure, he managed to **bounce back** with a new and successful project.*

*Despite the challenges, the team found a way to **bounce back** and achieve their goals.*

*She encouraged her friend to stay positive and **bounce back** from the disappointment.*

*It's inspiring to see how people can **bounce back** from adversity with resilience and determination.*

*He decided to focus on personal growth and development as a way to **bounce back** after a tough period.*

Cheese off

To annoy or irritate someone.

*His constant teasing really **cheesed off** his younger sister.*

*It's important not to do things that intentionally **cheese off** your colleagues in the workplace.*

*She was **cheesed off** by the noise coming from the construction site next door.*

*The repetitive questions started to **cheese off** the teacher.*

*They apologized for any actions that might have **cheesed off** their neighbors.*

Go for

To pursue or attempt; to choose or select.

*She decided to **go for** a jog to clear her mind after a stressful day.*

*They encouraged him to **go for** the job opportunity despite his initial hesitation.*

*He finally mustered the courage to **go for** his dream and start his own business.*

*It's essential to **go for** opportunities that align with your goals and aspirations.*

*She hesitated but ultimately decided to **go for** the adventurous option during the vacation.*

Feel down

To feel sad or depressed.

*After receiving the news, he couldn't help but **feel down** for a while.*

*They offered support and encouragement when their friend started to **feel down**.*

*She decided to take a break and do things she enjoyed to lift her spirits when she began to **feel down**.*

*It's important to reach out to friends or family when you start to **feel down** emotionally.*

*He acknowledged his emotions and took proactive steps to address why he was starting to **feel***

down.

Get rid of

To dispose of or eliminate something; to remove or discard.

> They decided to declutter their home and **get rid of** items they no longer needed.

> He wanted to **get rid of** old habits that were hindering his personal growth.

> She organized a garage sale to **get rid of** unused furniture and clothing.

> It's crucial to **get rid of** toxic relationships that negatively impact your well-being.

> They implemented a recycling program to responsibly **get rid of** waste in the community.

Wrap up

To complete or finish something; to conclude or bring to an end.

> They decided to **wrap up** the project ahead of

schedule due to their efficient teamwork.

*She asked the team to **wrap up** the meeting as they had covered all the agenda items.*

*He wanted to **wrap up** the day's tasks before heading home.*

*It's important to **wrap up** loose ends to ensure a smooth transition to the next phase.*

*They planned to **wrap up** the event with a closing ceremony and acknowledgments.*

Talk into

To persuade or convince someone to do something.

*She managed to **talk him into** joining the hiking trip despite his initial reservations.*

*They were successful in **talking** their friend **into** trying a new hobby.*

*He attempted to **talk her into** attending the social event with him.*

*It's important to use genuine and compelling reasons when trying to **talk someone into** a* *decision.*

*They decided to collaborate and **talk** their team **into** supporting a charitable cause.*

Hammer out

To negotiate or work out the details of an agreement or plan through discussion.

*They spent hours in the meeting room to **hammer out** the final details of the contract.*

*He called for a team meeting to **hammer out** the logistics for the upcoming project.*

*She believed in open communication to **hammer out** any issues within the team.*

*It's important to establish a collaborative environment to **hammer out** solutions to challenges.*

*They successfully **hammered out** a compromise that satisfied all parties involved.*

Follow up

To pursue or take further action after an initial contact or event.

> *After the job interview, he sent a thank-you email as a **follow-up** gesture.*
>
> *She made it a habit to **follow up** with clients to ensure their satisfaction with the products.*
>
> *They decided to **follow up** the initial meeting with a detailed proposal for the project.*
>
> *It's important to **follow up** on commitments and promises made to maintain trust.*
>
> *He scheduled a **follow-up** meeting to address any outstanding issues and ensure progress.*

Back down

To withdraw from a position, argument, or decision; to concede or yield.

> *After a lengthy debate, he chose to **back down** from his strong stance to find a compromise.*
>
> *They encouraged him not to **back down** from pursuing his goals despite challenges.*

*She decided to **back down** from the argument to maintain harmony within the team.*

*It's important to assess the situation and choose wisely when deciding to **back down** or stand firm.*

*They reached a mutual agreement after both parties were willing to **back down** on certain points.*

Waltz in

To enter a place casually and confidently, often in a bold or conspicuous manner.

*She decided to **waltz in** the meeting as if she owned the place.*

*He had the audacity to **waltz in** late to the class without any explanation.*

*They were surprised to see him **waltz in** unannounced to the party.*

*Despite the serious atmosphere, he chose to **waltz in** with a big smile.*

*She liked to **waltz in** with confidence to make a*

memorable entrance.

Fit in

To be socially accepted or to find a place where one belongs.

*It took a while for the new student to **fit in** with the rest of the class.*

*She always knew how to **fit in** seamlessly with different social groups.*

*He made an effort to **fit in** at the workplace by participating in team activities.*

*Despite being new to the city, she managed to **fit in** quickly and make friends.*

*It's important to create an inclusive environment where everyone can **fit in** comfortably.*

Talk up

To speak highly or enthusiastically about someone or something.

*She decided to **talk up** her colleague's*

achievements during the presentation.

*He always knew how to **talk up** the benefits of the product to potential clients.*

*They encouraged employees to **talk up** their ideas and contribute to team discussions.*

*Despite the challenges, she chose to **talk up** the positive aspects of the project.*

*He liked to **talk up** the strengths of his team members in front of senior management.*

Hash out

To discuss or resolve a problem, issue, or plan in detail through thorough conversation or negotiation.

*They scheduled a meeting to **hash out** the details of the upcoming project.*

*He wanted to **hash out** the differences and find a compromise with his colleague.*

*She believed in open communication to **hash out** any misunderstandings within the team.*

It's crucial to create a collaborative environment

*to **hash out** solutions to challenges.*

*They successfully **hashed out** a plan that satisfied all parties involved.*

Go under

To fail or become bankrupt; to sink or submerge underwater.

*Despite efforts to save the business, it eventually had to **go under**.*

*The company struggled financially and eventually **went under** due to mismanagement.*

*She feared that her small business might **go under** during the economic downturn.*

*It's important to take proactive measures to prevent a business from **going under**.*

*The ship encountered a severe storm and tragically **went under** in the rough seas.*

Be into

To have a strong interest or enthusiasm for
something.

*She's really **into** photography and spends hours
capturing beautiful moments.*

*He discovered a new hobby and quickly became
into it.*

*They were surprised to find out that their friend
was **into** collecting rare coins.*

*Despite his busy schedule, he always finds time to
pursue what he's **into**.*

*She decided to explore different activities to find
out what she's truly **into**.*

Get at

To imply, suggest, or express indirectly; to reach or
achieve.

*Despite the vague answer, he could sense there
was more she wanted to **get at**.*

*They were curious about what the author was
trying to **get at** with the mysterious ending.*

*She struggled to articulate her thoughts but eventually managed to **get at** the core issue.*

*It's important to listen carefully and understand what someone is trying to **get at** during a conversation.*

*He set clear goals and worked hard to **get at** the level of success he aspired to achieve.*

Take up with

To form a relationship or association with someone.

*Despite warnings, she decided to **take up with** a controversial artist.*

*He chose to **take up with** a group of like-minded individuals who shared his passion.*

*They were surprised when their friend decided to **take up with** a mysterious stranger.*

*It's important to be cautious when deciding to **take up with** someone new.*

*She decided to **take up with** a mentor who could guide her in her career.*

Set back

To delay or hinder progress; to cause a reversal or setback in plans.

> *The unexpected challenges **set back** the completion of the project by several weeks.*

> *Despite the setback, they remained determined to overcome the obstacles and **set back** their goals.*

> *She acknowledged the mistake that **set back** the team's progress and took responsibility.*

> *It's important to plan for contingencies to minimize the impact of setbacks that may **set back** a project.*

> *They faced a temporary **setback** but remained optimistic about achieving their long-term objectives.*

Drift apart

To gradually become less close or connected, especially in a relationship or friendship.

> *Despite being close in childhood, they started to **drift apart** as they pursued different paths in life.*

*She noticed that she and her friend were beginning to **drift apart** due to conflicting priorities.*

*They decided to address the issues that were causing them to **drift apart** in their relationship.*

*It's essential to invest time and effort in relationships to prevent them from **drifting apart**.*

*Despite the challenges, they managed to overcome differences and avoid **drifting apart** as friends.*

Buckle down

To apply oneself with determination and focus; to start working seriously on a task or goal.

*With exams approaching, she decided to **buckle down** and study for long hours.*

*He realized it was time to **buckle down** and finish the project before the deadline.*

*They encouraged the team to **buckle down** and meet the challenging targets set for the quarter.*

*Despite distractions, he managed to **buckle down** and complete the report ahead of schedule.*

*She knew she had to **buckle down** and focus on her fitness goals to see progress.*

Unit 4

Feel for

To empathize or sympathize with someone who is experiencing difficulty or hardship.

*She could **feel for** her friend going through a tough time and offered a listening ear.*

*He expressed how much he could **feel for** those affected by the natural disaster.*

*They showed genuine concern and **felt for** their colleague dealing with a personal loss.*

*Despite the differences, she could **feel for** the struggles of others and offer support.*

*He didn't just sympathize; he genuinely **felt for** those facing challenges in the community.*

Rile up

To provoke or stir up strong emotions, often anger or
annoyance.

*His controversial comments managed to **rile up** a
significant portion of the audience.*

*They intentionally avoided topics that could **rile
up** tensions during the family gathering.*

*She knew that discussing politics might **rile up**
some members of the group.*

*The provocative article was designed to **rile up**
readers and generate heated discussions.*

*Despite attempts to remain calm, the situation
continued to **rile up** emotions among the
participants.*

Live off

To rely on or sustain oneself using a particular source,
often related to finances or resources.

*After losing his job, he had to **live off** savings
until finding a new opportunity.*

*They decided to **live off** a simple lifestyle to save money for future endeavors.*

*She learned to **live off** the land, growing her own food and relying on sustainable practices.*

*Despite financial challenges, they found creative ways to **live off** limited resources.*

*He chose to **live off** freelance work, enjoying the flexibility it offered.*

Run into

To unexpectedly meet or encounter someone or something.

*While shopping, she happened to **run into** an old friend she hadn't seen in years.*

*They were surprised to **run into** each other at the airport, both on separate vacations.*

*He decided to take a different route only to **run into** a childhood acquaintance.*

*Despite the crowded event, they managed to **run into** each other and catch up.*

*She didn't expect to **run into** her former colleague at the local coffee shop.*

Level with

To be honest and straightforward with someone; to communicate openly and directly.

*She decided to **level with** her friend about the challenges she was facing.*

*They appreciated when people **leveled with** them, providing honest feedback.*

*He chose to **level with** his team about the current difficulties the company was facing.*

*Despite the potential consequences, she felt it was necessary to **level with** her supervisor.*

*They encouraged open communication and **leveling with** colleagues to foster a transparent work environment.*

Size up

To assess, evaluate, or analyze someone or

something, often to determine worth or suitability.

> *He took a moment to **size up** the competition before entering the business venture.*

> *They advised her to **size up** the situation carefully before making a decision.*

> *She had a keen ability to **size up** people, making her an effective judge of character.*

> *Before making an investment, he always took the time to **size up** the potential risks and rewards.*

> *Despite the initial impression, it's important to **size up** a situation from multiple perspectives.*

Pull out

To withdraw or remove something, often from a particular location or situation.

> *After the event, they decided to **pull out** of the partnership due to differences in vision.*

> *He warned investors to be cautious and consider the option to **pull out** if necessary.*

> *She had to make the tough decision to **pull out** of

the project to prioritize her health.

*Despite initial enthusiasm, they chose to **pull out** of the real estate investment before it became too risky.*

*It's crucial to have an exit strategy in place in case the need to **pull out** arises.*

Talk down to

To speak condescendingly or patronizingly to someone, often implying superiority.

*Despite being colleagues, he had a tendency to **talk down to** his team members.*

*She felt offended when others would **talk down to** her because of her age.*

*They made it a point never to **talk down to** new employees, fostering a supportive work culture.*

*He reminded everyone to communicate respectfully and avoid **talking down to** colleagues.*

*Despite his expertise, he never felt the need to **talk down to** others who were still learning.*

Swing by

To visit a place briefly or casually; to drop by or stop at a location.

*After work, she decided to **swing by** the grocery store to pick up a few things.*

*He promised to **swing by** the party for a short while, despite his busy schedule.*

*They invited friends to **swing by** their house for coffee and conversation.*

*Despite the rain, she made an effort to **swing by** the outdoor event to show her support.*

*He often liked to **swing by** the local bookstore to browse new releases.*

Fill up on

To eat or drink until satisfied or full.

*After the hike, they decided to **fill up on** a hearty meal at the local restaurant.*

*She tends to **fill up on** snacks before dinner, leaving little appetite for the main course.*

*Despite the tempting desserts, they chose to **fill up on** salads and vegetables.*

*He advised them not to **fill up on** too much water before the race to avoid discomfort.*

*During the holiday feast, it's easy to **fill up on** delicious treats and forget about the main course.*

Come around

To change one's opinion or attitude; to recover or regain consciousness.

*After much persuasion, he finally started to **come around** to the idea of a road trip.*

*She initially opposed the project, but eventually, she **came around** after seeing its benefits.*

*Despite initial resistance, he began to **come around** to the new policies implemented by the company.*

After fainting, it took a few minutes for her to

come around *and regain consciousness.*

*They patiently waited for their friend to **come around** and realize the importance of the decision.*

Look past

To ignore or disregard someone's faults or shortcomings; to focus on the positive aspects.

*Despite his flaws, she chose to **look past** them and appreciate his good qualities.*

*They encouraged the team to **look past** individual differences and work towards common goals.*

*He asked them to **look past** the mistakes and see the potential for growth in the project.*

*Despite the challenges, they managed to **look past** them and find solutions together.*

*It's important to **look past** superficial judgments and get to know people on a deeper level.*

Crank up

To increase the intensity or volume of something; to make something more powerful or active.

*As the party started, they decided to **crank up** the music for a lively atmosphere.*

*He suggested they **crank up** the speed during the workout to challenge themselves.*

*They decided to **crank up** the production of the new product to meet high demand.*

*Before the concert, they planned to **crank up** the energy by engaging the audience with interactive activities.*

*Despite the cold weather, they chose to **crank up** the intensity of the outdoor workout.*

Fight back

To resist or defend against an attack, criticism, or adversity; to attempt to overcome a challenge.

*Despite the setback, they decided to **fight back** and regain control of the situation.*

*She encouraged her friend to **fight back** against the unjust treatment they were facing.*

*He taught them how to **fight back** against negative thoughts and maintain a positive mindset.*

*They chose to **fight back** against the competition by innovating and offering unique products.*

*Despite the challenges, they were determined to **fight back** and achieve their goals.*

Slip out

To leave or exit quietly or unnoticed; to escape from a place.

*During the meeting, he decided to **slip out** to attend to an urgent matter.*

*She managed to **slip out** of the party without attracting much attention.*

*They planned to **slip out** of the office early to avoid traffic on the way home.*

Despite the crowded event, he successfully

__slipped out__ without anyone noticing.

He waited for the right moment to __slip out__ of the room without disrupting the conversation.

Rule out

To eliminate or exclude something as a possibility; to decide against.

After careful consideration, they decided to __rule out__ the option of outsourcing the project.

She recommended they __rule out__ certain candidates based on their lack of experience.

They agreed to __rule out__ a particular approach as it was deemed too risky.

Despite initial excitement, they chose to __rule out__ the idea due to practical constraints.

He suggested they carefully __rule out__ potential causes before making a final diagnosis.

Manage to

To succeed in doing something, often despite

challenges or difficulties.

> *Despite the tight deadline, they somehow **managed to** complete the project on time.*

> *She always found a way to **manage to** balance work and personal life effectively.*

> *They were surprised at how they **managed to** overcome obstacles and achieve success.*

> *Despite the odds, he **managed to** pursue his passion and build a successful career.*

> *Even with limited resources, they **managed to** create a memorable and impactful event.*

Bottle up

To suppress or restrain one's emotions, feelings, or thoughts; to keep something hidden or unexpressed.

> *She tended to **bottle up** her emotions, rarely expressing how she truly felt.*

> *He advised them not to **bottle up** their concerns but to communicate openly with each other.*

> *They noticed that he would **bottle up** his*

frustrations instead of addressing them directly.

*Despite the challenges, she chose not to **bottle up** her creativity and shared her ideas with the team.*

*It's important to create a supportive environment where individuals feel comfortable expressing themselves and not **bottling up** their emotions.*

Mooch off

To take advantage of someone by relying on their generosity, often without giving anything in return.

*He realized that his friend was starting to **mooch off** him, constantly asking for favors without reciprocating.*

*They decided to address the issue when they noticed a colleague trying to **mooch off** the team's hard work.*

*Despite their generosity, some individuals were known to **mooch off** the goodwill of others.*

*She learned to set boundaries and avoid allowing people to **mooch off** her kindness.*

It's important to maintain healthy relationships

*and avoid individuals who only seek to **mooch off** others.*

Iron out

To resolve or smooth out difficulties, conflicts, or issues; to make something clear or orderly.

*They scheduled a meeting to **iron out** the details of the upcoming project.*

*Despite initial disagreements, they managed to **iron out** a compromise that satisfied everyone.*

*He believed that open communication was essential to **iron out** misunderstandings within the team.*

*They spent hours trying to **iron out** the kinks in the new software before its release.*

*After weeks of negotiation, they finally were able to **iron out** the terms of the contract.*

Weigh in

To offer an opinion, perspective, or contribution; to

express one's views on a matter.

*During the discussion, each team member was encouraged to **weigh in** with their thoughts on the proposed changes.*

*He decided to **weigh in** on the debate, offering his insights and expertise.*

*They invited experts to **weigh in** on the environmental impact of the new construction project.*

*As a leader, she encouraged her team to **weigh in** on important decisions affecting the department.*

*It's crucial for all stakeholders to **weigh in** on the strategic planning process to ensure diverse perspectives.*

Set off

To start a journey or trip; to trigger or initiate an event or reaction.

*They decided to **set off** on a road trip to explore the scenic countryside.*

*The alarm clock is programmed to **set off** at 6 AM*

every morning.

*His announcement seemed to **set off** a chain reaction of excitement and anticipation in the room.*

*She carefully planned the surprise to **set off** a moment of joy and celebration.*

*As soon as the fireworks **set off**, the crowd erupted in cheers and applause.*

Bump up

To increase or raise something, such as a quantity, level, or price.

*They decided to **bump up** the budget to accommodate additional expenses.*

*The company chose to **bump up** production to meet the growing demand for their products.*

*Due to high demand, they decided to **bump up** the ticket prices for the upcoming concert.*

*She suggested a way to **bump up** the quality of the final product without increasing costs.*

*The unexpected surge in orders prompted them to **bump up** their manufacturing capabilities.*

Lay on

To organize or provide something.

*They decided to **lay on** a special celebration for the team's achievements.*

*The company planned to **lay on** a series of training sessions for employees.*

*As a gesture of appreciation, they chose to **lay on** a lavish dinner for their clients.*

*Despite the challenges, they managed to **lay on** a successful fundraising event for the charity.*

*She volunteered to **lay on** transportation for the team members attending the conference.*

Mess with

To interfere or tamper with; to engage in a confrontation or conflict with someone.

*He warned them not to **mess with** the settings on the computer without proper authorization.*

*Despite the disagreement, she chose not to **mess with** the delicate balance of the team dynamics.*

*They decided not to **mess with** the original recipe, fearing it might affect the taste.*

*She knew better than to **mess with** the intricate machinery without proper training.*

*He didn't want to **mess with** the established routines unless there was a clear benefit.*

Turn up

To arrive or appear, often unexpectedly; to increase in volume or intensity.

*She promised to **turn up** at the party despite her busy schedule.*

*They were surprised when an old friend decided to **turn up** at the reunion.*

*He suggested they **turn up** the music to create a more energetic atmosphere.*

*Despite the initial setback, their determination began to **turn up** as they faced challenges head-on.*

*The excitement in the room started to **turn up** as the event unfolded.*

Sleep in

To stay in bed and sleep later than usual; to have a late morning or leisurely start to the day.

*After a hectic week, they decided to **sleep in** and enjoy a relaxing Saturday morning.*

*She cherished the weekends as an opportunity to **sleep in** and recharge.*

*Despite the early alarm, they managed to **sleep in** on weekends to catch up on rest.*

*He looked forward to the holidays when he could **sleep in** without worrying about work commitments.*

*They agreed to **sleep in** on Sundays and spend quality time with family.*

Throw in

To add something extra, often without expecting compensation; to contribute or include something additional.

*As a bonus, they decided to **throw in** a complimentary gift with each purchase.*

*He offered to **throw in** his expertise at no additional cost to support the project.*

*They decided to **throw in** a surprise element to make the event more memorable.*

*She was generous enough to **throw in** some extra features as a gesture of goodwill.*

*Despite the tight budget, they managed to **throw in** some creative elements to enhance the overall experience.*

Come out

To be revealed or become known; to make a public appearance; to exit a place or position.

*The truth about the situation finally **came out** after weeks of speculation.*

*They decided to **come out** with the product launch despite some initial setbacks.*

*He encouraged his friend to **come out** and share their talent with the world.*

*After the intense meeting, it was a relief when the decision **came out** in their favor.*

*Despite the challenges, they were determined to **come out** stronger and more resilient.*

Tip off

To provide information or a warning, often discreetly; to alert or notify.

*He decided to **tip off** the authorities about the planned protest to ensure public safety.*

*She discreetly **tipped off** her friend about the surprise birthday party.*

*They received an anonymous phone call that **tipped off** the police about the illegal activity.*

*Despite the risks, he chose to **tip off** the media about the controversial issue.*

*It's essential to have reliable sources that can **tip off** you about potential opportunities or threats.*

Step in

To intervene or take action in a situation; to become involved or take over a role.

*When the conflict escalated, he had to **step in** and mediate between the parties involved.*

*She was asked to **step in** as the team leader during the manager's absence.*

*He decided to **step in** and assist when he saw someone struggling with a heavy load.*

*They had to **step in** and resolve the dispute before it affected the entire project.*

*It's crucial for leaders to know when to **step in** and provide guidance to their team.*

Root for

To support or cheer for someone or something; to wish for success.

*They gathered to **root for** their favorite team during the championship game.*

*Despite the challenges, her friends continued to **root for** her as she pursued her dreams.*

*He appreciated the encouragement and cheers from those who **rooted for** him during the competition.*

*Even in difficult times, it's important to have people who **root for** you and believe in your abilities.*

*They decided to **root for** the underdog, hoping for an unexpected victory.*

Poke around

To search or investigate casually and inquisitively; to explore or examine.

*Curious about the abandoned building, they decided to **poke around** and see what they could find.*

*She began to **poke around** in the attic, uncovering old family photographs and memorabilia.*

*He encouraged them to **poke around** the garden and discover the variety of plants and flowers.*

*Despite the warning signs, they couldn't resist the urge to **poke around** the mysterious cave.*

*They decided to **poke around** the online forums to gather information about the upcoming event.*

Set aside

To reserve or allocate something for a specific purpose; to save or keep aside.

*They agreed to **set aside** a portion of the budget for future unforeseen expenses.*

*She decided to **set aside** time each day for personal reflection and relaxation.*

*Despite the busy schedule, he made it a priority to **set aside** quality time with his family.*

*They chose to **set aside** differences and work collaboratively towards a common goal.*

*It's essential to **set aside** funds for emergency situations to ensure financial stability.*

End up

To eventually reach or result in a particular situation or outcome; to conclude or find oneself in a certain state.

*Despite the detour, they managed to **end up** at the scenic viewpoint they had heard about.*

*She never expected to **end up** in a career completely different from her original plan.*

*Despite the initial confusion, the project **ended up** being a great success.*

*He didn't plan to **end up** in that particular city, but circumstances led him there.*

*Despite the challenges, they were determined to **end up** with a product they could be proud of.*

Pile on

To add or increase something, often in a burdensome or overwhelming manner.

*The unexpected challenges seemed to **pile on** one after another, testing their resilience.*

*She felt the pressure **piling on** as the deadline for the exam approached.*

*Despite the setbacks, they continued to **pile on** efforts to overcome obstacles and succeed.*

*He warned them about the consequences of **piling on** too many tasks without proper planning.*

Stumble upon

To discover or find something unexpectedly or by chance.

*While hiking, they **stumbled upon** a hidden waterfall in the dense forest.*

*During their exploration, they **stumbled upon** an old, abandoned mansion with an intriguing history.*

*She was delighted to **stumble upon** a quaint bookstore during her visit to the unfamiliar town.*

They couldn't believe their luck when they
stumbled upon *a rare artifact at the flea market.*

Despite the initial aimlessness, they eventually
stumbled upon *a charming café with delicious*
pastries.

Be onto

To be aware of or suspicious about someone's actions
or intentions.

*He realized that his colleagues might **be onto** his*
plan to surprise them with a celebration.

Despite the attempts to conceal the truth, she
*suspected that others might **be onto** the*
deception.

They were careful not to leave any clues that
*would make others **onto** their secret project.*

*He had a feeling that someone might **be onto** his*
scheme to organize a surprise event.

Despite their efforts to be discreet, they couldn't
*shake the feeling that someone **was onto** their*
activities.

Draw up

To create or formulate a plan, document, or
agreement; to prepare or draft.

> They decided to **draw up** a detailed proposal
> before presenting the project to the client.

> Before starting the construction, they needed to
> **draw up** architectural plans for the new building.

> She worked late into the night to **draw up** a
> comprehensive business strategy for the
> upcoming year.

> They collaborated to **draw up** a contract that
> clearly outlined the terms and conditions.

> Before launching the campaign, they took the
> time to **draw up** a marketing plan to ensure its
> success.

Cap off

To complete or finish something in a satisfying or
notable way; to conclude an event or process.

> The award ceremony **capped off** a successful year
> for the team.

*They decided to **cap off** the evening with a spectacular fireworks display.*

*His remarkable achievement **capped off** a series of accomplishments throughout his career.*

*The celebratory dinner **capped off** the end of a challenging but rewarding project.*

*They chose to **cap off** the conference with an inspiring keynote speaker.*

Pop up

To appear suddenly or unexpectedly; to emerge or become noticeable.

*During the hike, a beautiful waterfall **popped up** around the bend.*

*Unexpected challenges **pop up** in every project, requiring adaptability and quick problem-solving.*

*As technology advances, new opportunities and trends **pop up** regularly.*

*He was surprised when an old friend **popped up** on his doorstep after years of no contact.*

*They witnessed a rare flower **popping up** in the garden, much to their delight.*

Talk down

To speak condescendingly or dismissively towards someone; to discourage or belittle.

*It's important not to **talk down** to colleagues, as it can create a negative work environment.*

*Instead of **talking down** to students, effective teachers encourage and empower them.*

*He regretted **talking down** to his team members during the stressful period.*

*Leadership involves guiding and supporting, rather than **talking down** to those under your supervision.*

*She never liked when people **talked down** to her based on her age.*

Bust in

To enter a place abruptly or forcefully, often without

permission.

> He **busted in** the room, demanding an explanation for the commotion.

> Despite the closed door, they **busted in** to find their friend in distress.

> They decided to **bust in** and surprise their colleague on their birthday.

> He regretted **busting in** on the private conversation without realizing the sensitivity of the topic.

> She laughed when her toddler **busted in** during an important virtual meeting.

Draw out

To extend the duration or length of something; to elicit information through conversation.

> They decided to **draw out** the meeting to address all concerns and suggestions.

> She skillfully **drew out** the details of the story during the interview.

*He deliberately **drew out** the suspense in the movie to captivate the audience.*

*They wanted to **draw out** the experience and make the most of their time together.*

*During the workshop, participants were encouraged to **draw out** their thoughts and ideas on paper.*

Round up

To gather or collect; to bring people or things together.

*They decided to **round up** volunteers for the community clean-up event.*

*He helped **round up** the team for a quick meeting to discuss the project updates.*

*Despite the challenges, they managed to **round up** enough participants for the charity run.*

*She quickly **rounded up** the necessary documents for the upcoming presentation.*

*They needed to **round up** the stray cattle that*

wandered into the neighborhood.

Sponge off

To rely on someone for support or resources without giving anything in return; to take advantage.

*He realized that his friend was starting to **sponge off** his generosity without reciprocating.*

*They confronted the colleague who seemed to **sponge off** the team's hard work.*

*Despite their kindness, some individuals were known to **sponge off** the goodwill of others.*

*She decided to distance herself from those who tried to **sponge off** her success.*

*They implemented measures to prevent people from **sponging off** the community's resources.*

Amp up

To increase or intensify something; to enhance or boost the strength or effectiveness.

*They decided to **amp up** their marketing efforts to*

reach a wider audience.

*As the competition grew fiercer, they needed to **amp up** their innovation to stay ahead.*

*He recommended strategies to **amp up** the energy and engagement during the event.*

*They agreed to **amp up** security measures to ensure the safety of the community.*

*She knew it was time to **amp up** her training regimen to prepare for the upcoming challenge.*

Prop up

To support or sustain something; to reinforce or provide assistance.

*They decided to **prop up** the leaning fence with additional posts.*

*He suggested using additional data to **prop up** the conclusions of the research.*

*She offered to **prop up** the struggling project by contributing her expertise.*

*They needed to find ways to **prop up** the*

declining economy.

*He decided to **prop up** the fragile vase with some hidden support.*

Sniff around

To investigate or explore in a casual or inquisitive manner; to look around for information.

*Curious about the noise, they decided to **sniff around** the abandoned warehouse.*

*Journalists often **sniff around** for stories that may be of public interest.*

*He started to **sniff around** the market to gather information about potential competitors.*

*She warned her friends not to **sniff around** her surprise birthday plans.*

*They encouraged students to **sniff around** various academic disciplines before choosing a major.*

Luck out

To experience good luck or fortune; to be fortunate or lucky.

> They really **luck out** when they found a rare collectible at the thrift store.

> Despite the odds, they managed to **luck out** and win the lottery.

> He felt that he **lucked out** with such a supportive and understanding team.

> She couldn't believe she **lucked out** and got the last ticket to the sold-out concert.

> They **lucked out** with perfect weather for their outdoor wedding.

Peer out

To look or gaze intently, especially from a concealed or restricted position.

> The curious cat **peered out** from behind the curtain to observe the visitors.

> She slowly **peered out** from her hiding place to see if the danger had passed.

*They decided to **peer out** of the window to catch a glimpse of the approaching parade.*

*He cautiously **peered out** to see who was knocking at the door.*

*The children giggled as they **peered out** from behind the bushes during hide-and-seek.*

Eat away

To erode, consume, or destroy gradually; to corrode or wear down over time.

*The constant exposure to moisture **ate away** at the wooden fence, causing it to weaken.*

*Over time, neglect can **eat away** at the foundations of even the strongest relationships.*

*They realized that stress was starting to **eat away** at their overall well-being.*

*Continuous exposure to acidic substances can **eat away** at the surface of metal objects.*

Plop down

To sit down heavily or abruptly; to drop or place something down with a dull sound.

*After a long day, she was eager to **plop down** on the comfortable sofa.*

*He **plopped down** on the grass, enjoying the warmth of the sun.*

*They decided to **plop down** at the picnic table for a quick lunch break.*

*The exhausted hiker finally **plopped down** on a rock to catch their breath.*

*After finishing the marathon, he gladly **plopped down** in a shaded area to rest.*

Shy away

To avoid or refrain from something due to fear, timidity, or reluctance.

*She tended to **shy away** from public speaking because of her fear of large audiences.*

*Despite the opportunity, he chose to **shy away***

from taking on additional responsibilities.

*They encouraged him not to **shy away** from expressing his creative ideas in the team.*

*People often **shy away** from discussing difficult topics to avoid confrontation.*

*She decided not to **shy away** from challenges and confront them head-on.*

Ponder over

To carefully think about or consider something; to reflect or contemplate.

*He needed some time to **ponder over** the important decision before making a choice.*

*She often liked to **ponder over** philosophical questions during quiet moments.*

*They decided to **ponder over** the options before deciding on the best course of action.*

*After the conversation, he took a walk to **ponder over** the insights shared by his friend.*

*It's important to **ponder over** the consequences of*

decisions before committing to them.

Home in on

To focus or move toward a target or objective with precision; to direct attention or effort.

> *The missile was programmed to **home in on** the target with remarkable accuracy.*

> *They decided to **home in on** specific issues during the discussion to find effective solutions.*

> *He knew how to **home in on** the key details that would make the presentation impactful.*

> *During the search, they used advanced technology to **home in on** the missing person's location.*

> *As the detective investigated the case, he started to **home in on** the likely suspects.*

Hone in on

To sharpen or refine a skill or ability; to improve or focus on a particular aspect.

*She decided to **hone in on** her communication skills to become a more effective leader.*

*They recognized the need to **hone in on** specific areas of the business to enhance efficiency.*

*He spent hours practicing to **hone in on** his guitar-playing technique.*

*As an athlete, he constantly worked to **hone in on** his speed and agility.*

*They encouraged employees to **hone in on** their strengths and develop expertise in their respective fields.*

Wise up

To become more knowledgeable or aware; to gain wisdom or insight.

*After the experience, he started to **wise up** about the importance of time management.*

*They decided to **wise up** about healthy eating habits for a better lifestyle.*

*It took a few setbacks for him to **wise up** and*

realize the value of hard work.

*She began to **wise up** about the impact of her actions on the environment.*

*As they faced challenges, the team members started to **wise up** and collaborate more effectively.*

Lawyer up

To hire or consult with a lawyer; to seek legal representation or advice.

*When faced with legal issues, it's essential to **lawyer up** to protect your rights.*

*They decided to **lawyer up** before entering into negotiations with the opposing party.*

*Despite the initial hesitation, they eventually chose to **lawyer up** to handle the legal complexities.*

*He realized the seriousness of the situation and quickly decided to **lawyer up** for proper guidance.*

Heat up

To increase in temperature; to make something warmer.

*She decided to **heat up** some leftovers for a quick dinner.*

*They used the microwave to **heat up** the soup.*

*As the sun set, the day started to **heat up** in preparation for a warm evening.*

*He suggested using the oven to **heat up** the frozen pizza.*

*She patiently waited for the tea kettle to **heat up** before making a cup of tea.*

Opt in

To choose to participate or be included in something; to actively select or agree to be part of a group or process.

*Users have the option to **opt in** for receiving promotional emails.*

*Before starting the service, customers can **opt in***

for additional features.

*He decided to **opt in** for the new software update to access the latest features.*

*Participants can **opt in** to receive notifications about upcoming events.*

*They were given the choice to **opt in** or opt out of the experimental study.*

See in

To welcome or usher in a new period or year; to celebrate the arrival of something.

*The community gathered to **see in** the New Year with a fireworks display.*

*They decided to host a party to **see in** the arrival of spring.*

*Family and friends joined together to **see in** the couple's anniversary.*

*As the clock struck midnight, everyone cheered to **see in** the beginning of a new era.*

*They lit candles to **see in** the festive season with*

warmth and joy.

Look in

To visit briefly; to stop by or check on someone or something.

> *She decided to **look in** on her elderly neighbor to make sure everything was okay.*

> *He promised to **look in** at the office during the weekend to catch up on work.*

> *They planned to **look in** on the construction site to monitor the progress.*

> *As they passed by the store, they decided to **look in** and browse the merchandise.*

> *She always makes it a point to **look in** on her favorite bookstore whenever she's in the area.*

Sit in

To attend or occupy a seat in a meeting, class, or gathering without actively participating; to be present as an observer or listener.

*She decided to **sit in** on the lecture to gain insights into the topic.*

*They allowed students to **sit in** on the conference to expose them to professional discussions.*

*As a journalist, he often had the opportunity to **sit in** on important press conferences.*

*She asked if she could **sit in** and observe the team meeting to understand their workflow.*

*He was invited to **sit in** on the board meeting to provide his expertise on the matter.*

Turn in

To submit or hand in something; to deliver or present for evaluation or approval.

*Students were required to **turn in** their assignments by the end of the week.*

*He worked late into the night to **turn in** the completed project before the deadline.*

*Participants were instructed to **turn in** their applications by the specified date.*

*She reminded everyone to **turn in** their feedback forms after the workshop.*

*They were excited to **turn in** their proposals for the upcoming competition.*

Opt out

To choose not to participate in something; to decline or withdraw from involvement.

*She decided to **opt out** of the company's wellness program due to personal reasons.*

*Participants have the option to **opt out** of receiving promotional emails.*

*He chose to **opt out** of the team-building event to focus on individual projects.*

*They were given the opportunity to **opt out** of the new policy if it didn't align with their values.*

*Despite the invitation, he decided to **opt out** of the social gathering.*

See out

To accompany or stay with someone until the end of a period or event.

*As a gesture of gratitude, he offered to **see out** his guests to their cars after the party.*

*She promised to **see out** her friend who was visiting from out of town until the last day.*

*He decided to **see out** the project, ensuring its successful completion.*

*They wanted to **see out** the elderly couple to make sure they safely reached their destination.*

*It's customary to **see out** departing colleagues with a farewell gathering.*

Watch out

To be cautious or vigilant; to pay attention to potential dangers or hazards.

*As they walked near the construction site, he warned his friend to **watch out** for falling debris.*

*Drivers are advised to **watch out** for pedestrians*

when approaching crosswalks.

*Parents tell their children to **watch out** for cars when playing near the street.*

*She reminded him to **watch out** for slippery surfaces after the rain.*

*During the hike, they were cautious and constantly told each other to **watch out** for uneven terrain.*

Click out

To exit or close a computer application or window by clicking on a button or icon.

*After finishing the document, she decided to **click out** of the word processing software.*

*Users can easily **click out** of the online platform by selecting the logout button.*

*He habitually saves his work before deciding to **click out** of the program.*

*It's important to properly **click out** of email accounts to ensure security.*

*Participants were instructed to **click out** of the webinar once the session concluded.*

Wash out

To clean or rinse thoroughly; to remove dirt, stains, or impurities through washing.

*After the outdoor activity, they needed to **wash out** the mud from their clothes.*

*She decided to **wash out** the paintbrushes after completing the art project.*

*Participants were advised to **wash out** their water bottles before refilling them.*

*He used a specialized shampoo to **wash out** the color from his hair.*

*It's essential to **wash out** food containers before recycling them.*

Dump out

To empty the contents of something quickly and forcefully; to pour out or discard in a hasty manner.

*He decided to **dump out** the contents of the bag to find his misplaced keys.*

*After finishing the project, they chose to **dump out** the unused materials.*

*She accidentally knocked over the container, causing it to **dump out** its contents.*

*It's quicker to **dump out** the puzzle pieces and assemble them on a flat surface.*

*He chose to **dump out** the old files to make room for new documents.*

Pour out

To cause a liquid to flow out of a container; to empty or release the contents of something.

*She carefully **poured out** the hot soup into bowls for the family.*

*As a symbolic gesture, they chose to **pour out** a drink in memory of their departed friend.*

*He decided to **pour out** his feelings in a heartfelt letter to his loved ones.*

*Participants were instructed to **pour out** the excess water after soaking the seeds.*

*They were amazed to watch the waterfall **pour out** over the edge of the cliff.*

Set out

To start a journey or a task; to begin a course of action or a specific plan.

*They woke up early to **set out** on their road trip across the country.*

*Before embarking on the adventure, they carefully **set out** their travel itinerary.*

*She decided to **set out** on a new career path after completing her education.*

*Participants were eager to **set out** on the hiking trail and explore the wilderness.*

*He carefully planned the steps before **setting out** to achieve his long-term goals.*

Let out

To allow something to escape or be released; to emit
or make a sound.

> *Upon opening the door, they accidentally **let out**
> the family cat.*

> *He couldn't help but **let out** a laugh when he
> heard the amusing story.*

> *She chose to **let out** her frustrations by screaming
> into a pillow.*

> *After holding it in for so long, he finally decided to
> **let out** his true feelings.*

> *They were surprised to hear the machine **let out** a
> loud beep to signal completion.*

Keep out

To prevent or prohibit entry; to maintain a barrier that
restricts access.

> *They put up a sign to remind people to **keep out**
> of the construction area.*

> *It's essential to **keep out** unwanted pests by*

sealing any gaps in the walls.

*He decided to install a security system to **keep out** intruders from his home.*

*Participants were instructed to **keep out** of the restricted zone for safety reasons.*

*She politely asked her siblings to **keep out** of her room while she was studying.*

Clip on

To attach or fasten something using a clip or clasp.

*She decided to **clip on** a decorative charm to her bracelet.*

*He quickly **clipped on** the safety light to his bicycle before riding at night.*

*Participants were instructed to **clip on** their name tags for the conference.*

*As the event started, the speaker chose to **clip on** a microphone for better amplification.*

*They were excited to **clip on** the badges that identified them as volunteers.*

Add on

To include or append something additional; to
supplement or extend.

*She decided to **add on** extra toppings to her pizza
for more flavor.*

*They offered customers the option to **add on**
accessories when purchasing electronics.*

*Participants were encouraged to **add on** an extra
day to their vacation for relaxation.*

*As the project progressed, they chose to **add on**
additional features to enhance its functionality.*

*He decided to **add on** a bonus chapter to the
book for readers who wanted more content.*

Cheer on

To encourage or support someone with cheers or
positive expressions.

*Friends and family gathered to **cheer on** the
marathon runners from the sidelines.*

He felt motivated when he heard his colleagues

__cheer on__ his successful presentation.

As the team faced a challenging game, fans continued to __cheer on__ their favorite players.

Participants were grateful for the crowd that came to __cheer on__ their efforts in the competition.

She decided to __cheer on__ her friend during the final stages of the talent show.

Sleep on

To postpone a decision or judgment until the next day or a later time; to think about something before taking action.

After the intense discussion, they decided to __sleep on__ the final decision and reconvene the next morning.

He preferred to __sleep on__ major choices to ensure clarity and avoid impulsive decisions.

As the deadline approached, she chose to __sleep on__ the project proposal before submitting it.

Participants were advised to __sleep on__ job offers before committing to a new position.

*They agreed to **sleep on** the negotiation terms to allow time for reflection.*

Keep on

To continue or persist in an action; to maintain ongoing effort.

*Despite the challenges, they decided to **keep on** working towards their goals.*

*He encouraged his team to **keep on** innovating and adapting to changing circumstances.*

*As the project faced setbacks, they were determined to **keep on** pushing forward.*

*Participants were motivated to **keep on** practicing for the upcoming competition.*

*She chose to **keep on** pursuing her passion despite the initial rejections.*

Drag on

To last for an extended or tedious period; to continue slowly or monotonously.

*The meeting seemed to **drag on** with endless discussions and little progress.*

*As they waited for the delayed flight, time seemed to **drag on** at the airport.*

*He found the lecture to be dull, making the hour **drag on** longer than usual.*

*Participants grew weary as the lengthy seminar seemed to **drag on** without a break.*

*Despite their efforts, the project timeline continued to **drag on** due to unforeseen challenges.*

Unit 5

Take on

To assume responsibility or a task; to accept a challenge or obligation.

*She decided to **take on** the leadership role to guide the team through the project.*

*As the company expanded, they needed to **take***

on new employees to handle increased workload.

He was eager to **take on** the challenging assignment to showcase his skills.

Participants were invited to **take on** additional roles during the event to enhance the experience.

Despite initial reservations, they agreed to **take on** the ambitious project with determination.

Leave on

To keep something activated or in a particular state when departing or not in use.

She preferred to **leave on** a soft light at night for a sense of security.

He accidentally chose to **leave on** the computer overnight, draining its battery.

Participants were reminded not to **leave on** electronic devices when not in use to save energy.

As they exited the room, they decided to **leave on** some background music for ambiance.

Despite the warm weather, she chose to **leave on**

the air conditioning for comfort.

Press on

To continue with determination or effort; to persevere in the face of challenges.

*Despite setbacks, they chose to **press on** and complete the project ahead of schedule.*

*He encouraged his team to **press on** even when the task seemed daunting.*

*As the deadline approached, participants were motivated to **press on** and meet their goals.*

*She decided to **press on** with her fitness routine despite feeling tired.*

*Despite the unexpected challenges, they were determined to **press on** and achieve success.*

Run on

To be powered or fueled by a particular energy source; to continue operating or functioning.

*The car was designed to **run on** electricity, reducing its environmental impact.*

*As the storm approached, the house relied on a generator to **run on** backup power.*

*He chose a laptop that could **run on** solar energy for more sustainable computing.*

*Participants were instructed to use devices that could **run on** battery power during the outdoor event.*

*The city buses were gradually transitioning to vehicles that could **run on** natural gas.*

Work on

To focus on or engage in a task or project; to make progress on a specific goal or objective.

*She decided to **work on** improving her communication skills for professional development.*

*He dedicated weekends to **working on** his novel, aiming to complete it by the end of the year.*

*As the team faced challenges, they collaborated to **work on** finding effective solutions.*

*Participants were encouraged to **work on** their strengths and weaknesses during the training program.*

*Despite distractions, they remained focused and continued to **work on** achieving their objectives.*

Egg on

To encourage or provoke someone to take a particular action, often negative or confrontational.

*He chose not to **egg on** his friend during the argument and instead diffused the tension.*

*Despite the disagreement, she decided not to **egg on** her colleague further.*

*Participants were reminded not to **egg on** conflict but rather seek resolution.*

*As the discussion became heated, he refrained from **egging on** any aggressive behavior.*

*They decided to walk away rather than **egg on***

the person causing the disturbance.

Nod off

To unintentionally fall asleep, especially in a sitting or relaxed position.

*After a long day at work, she started to **nod off** during the boring meeting.*

*While watching a movie, he began to **nod off** on the comfortable couch.*

*Participants in the meditation class sometimes **nod off** due to the calming atmosphere.*

*Despite trying to stay awake, she couldn't help but **nod off** during the lecture.*

*He often found himself **nodding off** during late-night study sessions.*

Tick off

To make a mark or check next to an item on a list; to irritate or annoy someone.

*She decided to **tick off** completed tasks on her to-*

do list for a sense of accomplishment.

*He unintentionally **ticked off** his colleague by forgetting to include them in the meeting.*

*Participants were asked to **tick off** their names on the attendance sheet upon entering the workshop.*

*Despite the attempt to be helpful, the suggestion seemed to **tick off** the team leader.*

*She carefully **ticked off** the items on the grocery list as she picked them up.*

Live off

To rely on something or someone for sustenance or support; to use as a means of survival.

*After losing his job, he had to **live off** his savings until he found a new opportunity.*

*They chose to **live off** the land, growing their own food and generating their energy.*

*Participants in the wilderness survival course had to learn how to **live off** limited resources.*

*During the difficult times, they had to **live off** the*

support of family and friends.

*Despite the challenges, she was determined to **live off** her passion for art.*

Call off

To cancel or terminate an event, activity, or arrangement.

*Due to inclement weather, they had to **call off** the outdoor concert.*

*He reluctantly had to **call off** the business meeting due to unforeseen circumstances.*

*Participants were informed that they needed to **call off** the team-building exercise for safety reasons.*

*She decided to **call off** the planned trip because of a family emergency.*

*Despite the preparations, they had to **call off** the wedding at the last minute.*

Pay off

To result in success or a positive outcome, especially after effort or investment.

*After years of hard work, their dedication to the project finally started to **pay off**.*

*Despite initial challenges, the decision to pursue higher education eventually **paid off**.*

*Participants in the fitness program saw their efforts **pay off** with improved health and well-being.*

*She hoped that her investment in the stock market would **pay off** in the long run.*

*Despite setbacks, the innovative approach to the problem eventually **paid off** with a breakthrough.*

Lay off

To terminate someone's employment; to suspend or cease an activity or process temporarily.

*Due to financial constraints, the company had to **lay off** several employees.*

*They decided to **lay off** production temporarily until the supply chain issues were resolved.*

*Participants were informed about the decision to **lay off** the project until further notice.*

*Despite efforts to avoid it, the organization had to **lay off** workers during the economic downturn.*

*He felt disheartened when he was told that the company would **lay off** a significant number of staff.*

Trade off

To exchange or sacrifice one thing for another; to make a compromise or balanced exchange.

*In negotiations, they had to **trade off** certain benefits to reach a mutually beneficial agreement.*

*He realized that in life, one often has to **trade off** immediate gratification for long-term success.*

*Participants were asked to consider the **trade-offs** between cost and quality in their decision-making.*

*She had to **trade off** some personal time to meet the tight deadlines at work.*

*Despite the challenges, they were willing to **trade off** convenience for a more sustainable lifestyle.*

Push off

To push away or depart from a place; to start or initiate a journey or activity.

*After saying their goodbyes, they decided to **push off** and begin their road trip.*

*He suggested they **push off** early to avoid traffic on their way to the event.*

*Participants were ready to **push off** on their kayaks and explore the scenic river.*

*Despite the rain, they chose to **push off** on their hiking adventure with enthusiasm.*

*She felt a sense of excitement as they prepared to **push off** on their sailing expedition.*

Show off

To display one's abilities, possessions, or achievements with pride in order to impress others.

*He couldn't resist the opportunity to **show off** his new guitar skills at the party.*

*Despite being modest, she decided to **show off** her art collection during the gallery opening.*

*Participants were encouraged to **show off** their creative projects during the showcase event.*

*She felt a sense of accomplishment and wanted to **show off** her latest completed project.*

*Despite the awkwardness, he couldn't resist the urge to **show off** his dance moves.*

Set off

To start a journey; to trigger or cause something to begin.

*They woke up early to **set off** on their road trip across the country.*

*Before embarking on the adventure, they carefully **set off** their travel itinerary.*

*She decided to **set off** on a new career path after completing her education.*

*Participants were eager to **set off** on the hiking trail and explore the wilderness.*

*He carefully planned the steps before **setting off** to achieve his long-term goals.*

Let off

To allow something to escape or be released; to emit or make a sound.

*Upon opening the door, they accidentally **let off** the family cat.*

*He couldn't help but **let off** a laugh when he heard the amusing story.*

*She chose to **let off** her frustrations by screaming into a pillow.*

*After holding it in for so long, he finally decided to **let off** his true feelings.*

*They were surprised to hear the machine **let off** a loud beep to signal completion.*

Go off

To explode or make a loud noise; to spoil or become rotten.

> *The fireworks started to **go off** in a spectacular display of colors and patterns.*

> *Despite careful preparation, the alarm accidentally **went off** and startled everyone in the room.*

> *Participants were warned about the importance of properly storing food to prevent it from **going off**.*

> *As the timer reached zero, the oven **went off**, indicating that the meal was ready.*

> *He accidentally dropped the glass, causing it to **go off** and shatter into pieces.*

Dry off

To remove moisture or wetness; to become dry after being wet.

> *After the rain stopped, they needed to **dry off** their clothes by the fireplace.*

*She used a towel to **dry off** after swimming in the pool.*

*Participants were advised to **dry off** thoroughly to avoid catching a cold in the chilly weather.*

*As they returned from the beach, they had to find a way to **dry off** before heading home.*

*Despite the unexpected rain, they found a cozy spot to **dry off** and enjoy their picnic.*

Fight off

To defend against or resist an attack, threat, or challenge.

*Despite feeling unwell, he tried to **fight off** the flu by getting plenty of rest.*

*She had to **fight off** negative thoughts and stay focused on her goals.*

*Despite feeling exhausted, she fought to stay awake and **fight off** sleepiness.*

Look after

To take care of or attend to someone or something; to be responsible for their well-being.

*She always makes sure to **look after** her younger siblings when their parents are away.*

*As a pet owner, it's important to **look after** the needs and health of your animals.*

*Participants were reminded to **look after** their belongings during the outdoor excursion.*

*He volunteered to **look after** his neighbor's plants while they were on vacation.*

*She promised to **look after** her friend who wasn't feeling well.*

Take after

To resemble or inherit certain traits, characteristics, or behaviors from a family member.

*He **takes after** his mother in terms of artistic talent and creativity.*

*She noticed that her daughter seemed to **take***

after her love for reading and learning.

Participants shared stories about how they **take after** their grandparents in various aspects.

Despite being adopted, the child began to **take after** his adoptive parents in personality.

He was proud to see his son **take after** him in his passion for sports.

Run around

To move quickly or energetically in various directions; to engage in activities or errands.

The children love to **run around** in the backyard, playing games and laughing.

During the festival, people can be seen **running around** to different booths and attractions.

Participants were encouraged to take a break and **run around** to stretch their legs.

Despite the busy schedule, she always finds time to let her dog **run around** in the park.

He remembered the days when he and his friends

*used to **run around** the neighborhood after school.*

Chase after

To pursue or follow closely in an effort to catch or reach someone or something.

*During the game of tag, the children would **chase after** each other with excitement.*

*She had to **chase after** the bus as it started to pull away from the stop.*

*Participants were amused to see the playful puppy **chase after** its own tail in the yard.*

*Despite the rain, they decided to **chase after** the rainbow that appeared in the sky.*

*He had to **chase after** his hat that was blown away by the strong wind.*

Go after

To pursue or seek something, such as a goal, dream, or opportunity.

*She was determined to **go after** her dream of becoming a professional dancer.*

*He decided to **go after** a career in science after discovering his passion for research.*

*Participants were inspired to **go after** their goals and not be afraid of challenges.*

*Despite facing setbacks, they continued to **go after** the project with unwavering dedication.*

*She encouraged her friends to **go after** opportunities that aligned with their interests and values.*

Get after

To scold or reprimand someone for their behavior or actions; to urge or motivate.

*She had to **get after** her children to complete their homework before dinner.*

*He constantly **got after** his team to maintain high standards of performance.*

Participants were reminded that constructive

feedback is a way to **get after** improvement.

Despite the challenges, the coach continued to **get after** the players to give their best on the field.

She chose to **get after** herself to stay disciplined and focused on her goals.

Come before

To precede or be more important or significant than something else.

He believed that family should always **come before** personal achievements.

Participants were reminded that safety should **come before** speed in any physical activity.

She prioritized honesty and integrity to **come before** any professional success.

They learned that establishing trust should **come before** attempting to implement major changes.

He emphasized that the well-being of employees should always **come before** profit margins.

Put before

To prioritize or place something as more important than another.

*She always tried to **put family before** career aspirations in her decision-making.*

*Despite the tempting offer, he chose to **put ethics before** personal gain.*

*Participants were encouraged to **put health before** work demands to maintain a balanced lifestyle.*

*They discussed the importance of **putting safety before** speed when driving in adverse conditions.*

*He believed in **putting integrity before** success in his professional life.*

Go before

To precede or come before someone or something in time, order, or importance.

*Traditional values and customs often **go before** modern influences in their community.*

*She believed that taking care of one's mental health should **go before** other priorities.*

*Participants were reminded that proper planning should **go before** execution in any project.*

*They discussed how collaboration and teamwork should always **go before** individual achievements.*

*He emphasized the principle that safety should **go before** speed in any activity.*

Close down

To permanently cease the operation or existence of a business, organization, or place.

*Due to financial challenges, the company had to **close down** its manufacturing facility.*

*He decided to **close down** the small bookstore as online shopping became more popular.*

*Participants were saddened by the news that the local restaurant would **close down** after many years in business.*

*The decision to **close down** the community center*

Wear down

To gradually reduce the strength or effectiveness of someone or something through continuous use or friction.

Track down

To locate or find someone or something, often after a
search or investigation.

*Detectives worked tirelessly to **track down** the
suspect involved in the robbery.*

*Despite the anonymity, they managed to **track
down** the author of the viral online post.*

*Participants were challenged to use clues and
information to **track down** the hidden treasure.*

*She hired a private investigator to help her **track
down** her long-lost relatives.*

*With the use of advanced technology, they were
able to **track down** the missing shipment.*

Tear down

To demolish or dismantle a structure or object,
typically a building.

*The city decided to **tear down** the old bridge and
construct a more modern one.*

*They needed to **tear down** the dilapidated house*

to make way for a new development.

*Participants were informed about the plans to **tear down** the abandoned factory in the neighborhood.*

*Environmental concerns led to the decision to **tear down** the outdated power plant.*

*He hired a demolition crew to **tear down** the unsafe structure on his property.*

Run down

To decline in condition, energy, or functionality; to become worn out or exhausted.

*The old car began to **run down** and required frequent repairs.*

*They noticed that the town had started to **run down** over the years, with neglected buildings and infrastructure.*

*Participants were advised to take breaks to avoid feeling **run down** during the demanding training program.*

*The continuous workload began to **run down** the*

team, affecting their productivity.

*Despite being passionate about the project, she felt herself starting to **run down** due to the constant stress.*

Narrow down

To reduce the number of options or possibilities; to make something more specific or focused.

*They needed to **narrow down** the list of candidates for the job position.*

*After hours of discussion, the team managed to **narrow down** the potential solutions to the problem.*

*Participants were encouraged to **narrow down** their research topics for the upcoming project.*

*She decided to **narrow down** her choices when selecting a college for her studies.*

*Through careful analysis, they were able to **narrow down** the source of the issue to a specific component.*

Let down

To disappoint or fail someone; to not meet the
expectations or hopes of someone.

> *She felt deeply hurt when her friend **let her down**
> by breaking their promise.*
>
> *Despite their efforts, the team couldn't avoid
> **letting down** their supporters in the
> championship.*
>
> *Participants were asked not to **let down** their
> teammates by missing crucial deadlines.*
>
> *He was determined not to **let down** his family by
> making responsible decisions.*
>
> *She apologized sincerely for any instance where
> she might have **let down** her colleagues.*

Keep down

To control or maintain at a lower level; to prevent
something from rising or increasing.

> *Regular exercise and a healthy diet can help **keep
> down** cholesterol levels.*

*The company implemented cost-cutting measures to **keep down** expenses during tough times.*

*Participants were advised to drink water to **keep down** their body temperature during the intense workout.*

*He took medication to **keep down** the symptoms of his allergies.*

*They worked together to **keep down** noise levels during the important meeting.*

Crack down on

To take strict action to stop or control a particular activity; to enforce rules rigorously.

*The government decided to **crack down on** illegal gambling activities in the city.*

*Law enforcement agencies collaborated to **crack down on** drug trafficking in the region.*

*Participants were warned about the consequences if they didn't **crack down on** safety violations.*

They implemented new security measures to

crack down on *unauthorized access to the building.*

The school decided to **crack down on** *bullying behavior to create a safer environment.*

Cut down

To reduce the quantity or amount of something; to decrease or lessen.

As part of their environmental initiative, the company decided to **cut down** *on paper usage.*

He made a conscious effort to **cut down** *on sugary snacks to improve his health.*

Participants were encouraged to find ways to **cut down** *on unnecessary expenses in their budget.*

They planned to **cut down** *the meeting duration to make it more efficient.*

She decided to **cut down** *on screen time and spend more time outdoors.*

Hold down

To maintain a job or position; to fulfill the responsibilities of a role.

> Despite the challenges, she managed to **hold down** a demanding job and take care of her family.

> He worked hard to **hold down** the position of team captain through consistent performance.

> Participants were encouraged to develop the skills necessary to **hold down** leadership roles.

> Despite being a rookie, she proved her ability to **hold down** a spot in the starting lineup.

> He faced difficulties but continued to **hold down** his role as the head of the department.

Hold out for

To wait for the best possible outcome or deal; to insist on getting the best result.

> She decided to **hold out for** a higher salary before accepting the job offer.

> Despite tempting offers, they chose to **hold out for** the best terms in the contract negotiation.

*Participants were advised to **hold out for** the most favorable conditions in their business deals.*

*He believed in the importance of **holding out for** the right opportunity rather than rushing into decisions.*

*They decided to **hold out for** a better price when selling their property.*

Hold back from

To refrain or prevent oneself from doing something; to resist taking a particular action.

*Despite the temptation, he managed to **hold back from** indulging in unhealthy snacks.*

*She had to **hold back from** expressing her opinion during the heated discussion.*

*Participants were encouraged to **hold back from** making impulsive decisions in high-pressure situations.*

*He struggled to **hold back from** reacting emotionally to the criticism.*

Rip up

To tear into pieces or destroy something, typically a piece of paper or document.

*He decided to **rip up** the old contract and create a new one with updated terms.*

*She was so frustrated with the draft that she chose to **rip up** the entire manuscript.*

*Participants were asked not to **rip up** any important documents and to handle them with care.*

*Despite the anger, he resisted the urge to **rip up** the letter and chose to respond calmly.*

*They accidentally **ripped up** the wrong document and had to piece it back together.*

Sign up

To enroll or register for something; to commit to

participating in an activity or event.

> *She decided to **sign up** for the dance classes to pursue her passion for dancing.*

> *They encouraged employees to **sign up** for professional development workshops to enhance their skills.*

> *Participants were eager to **sign up** for the charity run to support a good cause.*

> *He decided to **sign up** for the language course to improve his communication skills.*

> *Despite the initial hesitation, she eventually chose to **sign up** for the volunteer program.*

Mix up

To confuse or combine things in a way that makes it difficult to distinguish them.

> *He accidentally **mixed up** the files, causing confusion in the office.*

> *She tends to **mix up** similar-sounding words, leading to humorous misunderstandings.*

*Participants were warned not to **mix up** the chemicals in the laboratory to avoid accidents.*

*Despite their efforts, they accidentally **mixed up** the order of the presentations during the conference.*

*They realized they had **mixed up** the dates for the important meeting and had to reschedule.*

Clog up

To block or obstruct a passage, system, or flow, causing it to become congested or jammed.

*Leaves and debris from the storm began to **clog up** the gutters, causing water damage.*

*Heavy traffic during rush hour tends to **clog up** the main streets in the city.*

*Participants were advised not to dispose of items that could **clog up** the plumbing system.*

*The accumulation of snow and ice can **clog up** the ventilation system of a vehicle.*

*They realized that outdated software could **clog***

up the computer system and slow down operations.

Tape up

To use tape to close or secure something; to apply tape to repair or mend.

*They decided to **tape up** the ripped pages of the book to prevent further damage.*

*Participants were asked to **tape up** any exposed wires to ensure safety in the workshop.*

*He had to **tape up** the torn packaging to keep the contents intact during transit.*

*Despite the temporary fix, they managed to **tape up** the leaking pipe until a plumber arrived.*

*She chose to **tape up** the torn seams of her backpack before embarking on the hiking trip.*

Lace up

To fasten or tie shoelaces securely.

*Before the game, the athletes needed to **lace up***

their cleats to ensure a proper fit.

*She took a moment to **lace up** her running shoes before heading out for a jog.*

*Participants were instructed to **lace up** their hiking boots tightly for a safe and comfortable trek.*

*He reminded the team to **lace up** their skates before stepping onto the ice rink.*

*Despite the rain, they decided to **lace up** their sneakers for a refreshing walk in the park.*

Hike up

To increase the price or cost of something, often unexpectedly or significantly.

*The company decided to **hike up** the prices of its products due to increased production costs.*

*Unexpected demand for the concert tickets led the organizers to **hike up** the ticket prices.*

*Participants were concerned when they learned about the plan to **hike up** membership fees.*

*Market conditions forced the airline to **hike up** the prices of its flight tickets.*

*They were disappointed when the landlord decided to **hike up** the rent for the apartment.*

Set up

To arrange or establish something; to prepare or organize.

*They decided to **set up** a new business to pursue their entrepreneurial dreams.*

*Participants were instructed on how to **set up** the equipment for the upcoming event.*

*He worked hard to **set up** a meeting with potential investors for the project.*

*She helped **set up** a charity event to raise funds for a local cause.*

*Before the conference, they needed to **set up** the exhibition booth to showcase their products.*

Clear up

To make something tidy or free from clutter; to resolve or clarify a situation.

*She decided to **clear up** her desk before starting a new project.*

*After the storm, they worked together to **clear up** the fallen branches and debris in the yard.*

*Participants were asked to **clear up** any misunderstandings before proceeding with the team project.*

*He made an effort to **clear up** the confusion by providing detailed explanations.*

*They decided to **clear up** the storage room to create more space for supplies.*

Wrap up

To conclude or finish something; to complete the final details.

*As the project neared its end, they began to **wrap up** the remaining tasks.*

*Participants were reminded to **wrap up** their presentations within the allotted time.*

*He decided to **wrap up** the day's work and head home early.*

*She needed to **wrap up** the report before the deadline approached.*

*Before leaving, they took a few minutes to **wrap up** the discussion and summarize key points.*

Work up

To build up or develop gradually; to create or generate.

*They decided to **work up** their strength by gradually increasing their workout intensity.*

*He needed to **work up** the courage to speak in front of a large audience.*

*Participants were encouraged to **work up** a plan for the upcoming project.*

*She wanted to **work up** her skills in photography by practicing regularly.*

*They aimed to **work up** enthusiasm for the new product launch through effective marketing.*

Turn up

To appear or arrive unexpectedly; to increase the volume or intensity.

*He decided to **turn up** at the party even though he wasn't initially planning to attend.*

*Despite the forecast, the weather took a pleasant turn, and the sun decided to **turn up**.*

*Participants were surprised when a famous musician decided to **turn up** and perform at the event.*

*She wanted to **turn up** the music to create a lively atmosphere at the gathering.*

*As the excitement grew, they decided to **turn up** the intensity of the celebration.*

Run up

To accumulate or increase quickly; to sprint or jog

towards something.

> *Unexpected expenses began to **run up** and put a strain on their budget.*

> *He had to **run up** the stairs to catch the train that was about to depart.*

> *Participants were warned not to **run up** excessive debts on their credit cards.*

> *She realized she needed to **run up** her savings for the upcoming vacation.*

> *They decided to **run up** the flag to signal the start of the event.*

Make up

To invent or create; to reconcile after a disagreement; to apply cosmetics.

> *She had to **make up** a story to explain her absence during the meeting.*

> *After the argument, they decided to **make up** and put the disagreement behind them.*

> *Participants were encouraged to **make up** their

own creative solutions to the problem.

*He needed to **make up** time after being delayed in traffic.*

*She spent some time in front of the mirror to **make up** before the important presentation.*

Hand over

To give or transfer something to someone else, typically after a request or demand.

*He was asked to **hand over** the documents to the authorities for further examination.*

*Participants were instructed to **hand over** their completed assignments before leaving the classroom.*

*She decided to **hand over** the responsibilities of the project to her capable team members.*

*Before the meeting, they needed to **hand over** the presentation materials to the event organizers.*

*They reluctantly agreed to **hand over** the keys to the rental car at the end of their trip.*

Knock over

To cause something to fall over by striking it; to collide with and overturn an object or person.

> *Strong winds threatened to **knock over** the tall street lamps along the boulevard.*
>
> *He accidentally **knocked over** the stack of books while reaching for a volume on the top shelf.*
>
> *Participants were warned not to **knock over** the fragile display of glassware in the exhibition hall.*
>
> *She apologized after her dog playfully **knocked over** a small child in the park.*
>
> *Despite the caution signs, a distracted driver managed to **knock over** a traffic cone on the road.*

Look over

To examine or inspect something; to review or consider carefully.

> *She took a moment to **look over** the contract before signing it to ensure all terms were acceptable.*

*Before submitting the report, they decided to **look over** it for any potential errors or improvements.*

*Participants were encouraged to **look over** the agenda for the meeting and provide feedback.*

*He needed to **look over** the blueprints before starting construction on the new building.*

*They took the time to **look over** the menu and decide what to order at the restaurant.*

Run over

To hit with a vehicle and pass over; to exceed a time limit; to review or summarize quickly.

*He narrowly avoided a collision when a cyclist unexpectedly **ran over** the road.*

*She apologized after accidentally **running over** her friend's foot with the shopping cart.*

*Participants were warned not to **run over** the allocated time for their presentations.*

*He needed to **run over** the main points of the speech before delivering it to the audience.*

*Despite being in a rush, they decided not to **run over** the speed limit on the highway.*

Stop over

To make a short stay during a journey; to pause or break a journey temporarily.

*They decided to **stop over** in a quaint town for a quick lunch on their road trip.*

*She often chose to **stop over** at the airport lounge during long layovers.*

*Participants were advised to **stop over** at the rest area to stretch their legs during the long bus ride.*

*Before reaching the final destination, they planned to **stop over** in a scenic location for sightseeing.*

*Despite the tight schedule, they managed to **stop over** at a historic landmark on their journey.*

Turn over

To change the side or position of something; to

transfer or give control or responsibility to someone else.

> *She decided to **turn over** the mattress to ensure even wear and comfort.*

> *Before the negotiation, they needed to **turn over** all relevant documents to the legal team.*

> *Participants were instructed to **turn over** their answer sheets once they had completed the exam.*

> *He felt it was time to **turn over** the leadership of the project to a more experienced team member.*

> *Despite the challenges, they managed to **turn over** the company's financial situation in a short period.*

Sleep over

To spend the night at a place; to stay overnight as a guest.

> *They invited their friends to **sleep over** and enjoy a movie marathon at their house.*

> *Before the big event, participants were allowed to **sleep over** at the venue to ensure an early start*

the next day.

*She decided to **sleep over** at her cousin's place to avoid the late-night commute.*

*Despite the storm, they welcomed their guests to **sleep over** and wait for better weather conditions.*

*He often invited his close friends to **sleep over** during the weekends for a mini-getaway.*

Take over

To assume control, responsibility, or possession; to become dominant or prevalent.

*After the retirement, he decided to **take over** the family business and continue the legacy.*

*They needed a new manager to **take over** the team and lead them to success.*

*Participants were excited about the opportunity to **take over** the planning of the annual event.*

*She decided to **take over** the responsibilities of the project coordinator during their absence.*

Despite the challenges, the new technology began

to **take over** the market quickly.

Make over

To change or improve the appearance or function of something or someone; to undergo a transformation.

*She decided to **make over** her bedroom by painting the walls and getting new furniture.*

*Before the makeover show, the team worked hard to **make over** the outdated living space.*

*Participants were excited about the opportunity to **make over** their personal style with the help of fashion experts.*

*He suggested they **make over** the website to enhance user experience and attract more visitors.*

*Despite initial skepticism, the old building underwent a remarkable **makeover** and became a modern office space.*

Go over

To review, examine, or discuss in detail; to move from

one side to another.

> *Before the presentation, they decided to **go over** the key points to ensure a smooth delivery.*

> *She asked her teacher to **go over** the challenging concepts from the lesson for better understanding.*

> *Participants were encouraged to **go over** the safety guidelines before starting the experiment.*

> *He took a moment to **go over** the contract and address any concerns before signing it.*

> *Despite the tight schedule, they decided to **go over** the project timeline to identify potential delays.*

Skip over

To omit or bypass; to jump or pass over something without paying attention to it.

> *During the presentation, he chose to **skip over** the less relevant details and focus on the main points.*

> *She decided to **skip over** the introductory chapters of the book and get straight to the main*

storyline.

Participants were reminded not to **skip over** any steps in the instructions to avoid mistakes.

He encouraged his team to **skip over** the unnecessary bureaucracy and work efficiently.

Despite the long list of tasks, they decided to **skip over** the less urgent ones and prioritize the critical ones.

Come under

To experience or undergo something; to be subjected to scrutiny or examination; to fall within a specific category, area of authority, or responsibility.

The city **came under** attack during the war.

The company's practices **came under** scrutiny after reports of unethical behavior.

This issue **comes under** the responsibility of the finance department.

The new department will **come under** the management of the Vice President.

Fall under

To be subject to or be included in a particular category or rule.

> *The newly introduced policy would affect all projects that **fall under** the infrastructure category.*

> *Participants were reminded that their work would **fall under** the guidelines set by the regulatory authority.*

> *Projects that **fall under** the research and development department receive additional funding.*

Put under

To subject to a particular treatment, influence, or condition.

> *The new employees were **put under** a comprehensive training program to familiarize them with company procedures.*

> *Participants were concerned about being **put under** increased pressure due to the upcoming project deadlines.*

Go under

To fail or go bankrupt; to sink or submerge.

*The economic downturn caused many businesses to **go under** despite their efforts to stay afloat.*

*They were worried about the possibility of their company **going under** due to financial challenges.*

*Participants discussed strategies to prevent the organization from **going under** in the competitive market.*

*Small businesses faced the risk of **going under** if they couldn't adapt to the changing market conditions.*

*The boat started to take on water, and there was a real risk of it **going under** if not addressed immediately.*

Pass through

To move or travel through a place or region; to go by or across.

*As a tourist, they had the opportunity to **pass***

***through** various cities and experience different cultures.*

*Participants were advised to carry proper identification when they **pass through** airport security.*

*During the road trip, they would **pass through** picturesque landscapes and charming small towns.*

*He decided to **pass through** the bustling market to explore local products.*

*Trains would regularly **pass through** the station on their way to different destinations.*

Break through

To overcome obstacles or barriers; to make a significant advance or progress.

*Despite challenges, they managed to **break through** and achieve success in their endeavors.*

*Participants were excited about the possibility of their innovative ideas **breaking through** in the market.*

*They worked tirelessly to **break through** the language barrier and communicate effectively.*

*After years of hard work, the research team was able to **break through** and make groundbreaking discoveries.*

*She encouraged her team to stay persistent and **break through** any setbacks they encountered.*

Fall through

To fail to happen or be completed as planned; to collapse or be abandoned.

*The original plans for the event had to **fall through** due to unforeseen circumstances.*

*Despite initial excitement, the business deal eventually **fell through** during negotiations.*

*Participants were disappointed when the scheduled outdoor activity had to **fall through** because of bad weather.*

*They had high hopes for the project, but it ultimately **fell through** due to lack of funding.*

*She was upset when her plans to travel **fell through** at the last minute.*

Unit 6

Get through with

To complete or finish something; to successfully accomplish a task or activity.

*After hours of hard work, they were finally able to **get through with** the complex project.*

*Participants were relieved to **get through with** the challenging exam and move on to the next stage.*

*He was determined to **get through with** the marathon, despite the difficult terrain.*

*She focused on her studies to **get through with** the semester with good grades.*

*They celebrated when they could finally **get through with** the construction of their dream house.*

Go through with

To proceed with or carry out a plan, action, or decision, especially when facing difficulties or doubts.

*Despite the challenges, they decided to **go through with** the ambitious project.*

*Participants were encouraged to have confidence and **go through with** their innovative ideas.*

*He hesitated but ultimately chose to **go through with** the challenging surgery for his health.*

*She was determined to **go through with** the business expansion despite economic uncertainties.*

*They discussed the potential risks but still decided to **go through with** the risky investment.*

Pull through

To recover from an illness or difficulty; to survive a challenging situation.

*Despite the severity of the accident, he managed to **pull through** and regain his health.*

*Participants were grateful for the support that helped them **pull through** a tough period.*

*She faced a life-threatening illness but miraculously managed to **pull through** with the help of medical treatment.*

*Despite the odds, they were determined to help each other **pull through** the economic challenges.*

*With determination and support, they were able to **pull through** the emotional strain of the situation.*

Skim through

To read or look at something quickly and not very thoroughly; to glance through.

*She didn't have much time, so she decided to **skim through** the report to get the main points.*

*Participants were asked to **skim through** the documents before the meeting for a brief overview.*

*He quickly **skimmed through** the textbook to*

find the relevant information for his presentation.

*Despite the lengthy document, they were able to **skim through** it and identify the key findings.*

*Before the interview, she decided to **skim through** the company's website to gather some background information.*

Tack on

To add or attach something, often quickly or informally.

*Before submitting the proposal, they decided to **tack on** a few additional points to strengthen their case.*

*Participants were asked to **tack on** any last-minute updates to their presentations before the conference.*

*He suggested they **tack on** a special discount to the final offer to make it more appealing.*

*Despite the tight schedule, they managed to **tack on** an extra meeting to discuss urgent matters.*

*She decided to **tack on** a personal note to the end of the email for a more friendly touch.*

Pile on

To add or increase something, often in a large quantity; to intensify or accumulate.

*As the project progressed, they had to **pile on** additional resources to meet the tight deadline.*

*Participants were warned not to **pile on** unnecessary details in their reports and focus on key information.*

*Despite efforts to simplify the process, they continued to **pile on** more steps, making it confusing for users.*

*During the holiday season, they tended to **pile on** extra workload to meet increased demand.*

*She realized it was time to delegate tasks as the responsibilities began to **pile on**.*

Try on

To put on or wear something to see how it looks or fits; to test or experience.

*Before buying the dress, she decided to **try on** different sizes to find the perfect fit.*

*Participants were encouraged to **try on** the virtual reality headset to experience the new simulation program.*

*He needed to **try on** the new running shoes before making a purchase to ensure comfort.*

*Despite initial hesitation, they decided to **try on** the new software to evaluate its features.*

*She enjoyed going to the store and spending time **trying on** various outfits for different occasions.*

Decide on

To make a choice or reach a decision after careful consideration.

*After reviewing the options, they were able to **decide on** the best course of action for the project.*

*Participants were given time to **decide on** their preferred workshop sessions for the conference.*

*He asked for everyone's input before they could collectively **decide on** the team's goals for the upcoming year.*

*Despite the differing opinions, they managed to **decide on** a color scheme for the office renovation.*

*She took the weekend to **decide on** whether to accept the job offer or explore other opportunities.*

Cheat on

To be unfaithful in a relationship; to betray someone by breaking a commitment.

*Despite their vows, he chose to **cheat on** his spouse, causing significant pain in the relationship.*

*Participants discussed the consequences of choosing to **cheat on** their colleagues in a team project.*

*She was devastated when she discovered her partner had been attempting to **cheat on** her with a co-worker.*

*Despite the temptations, they remained committed and chose not to **cheat on** each other.*

*He regretted the decision to **cheat on** his business partner, as it led to the dissolution of their partnership.*

Lie on

To recline or rest on a surface; to be located or situated on.

*After a long day, she decided to **lie on** the couch and relax for a while.*

*Participants were instructed to **lie on** the yoga mats for the final relaxation exercise.*

*He enjoyed finding a sunny spot in the park to **lie on** and read a book.*

*Despite the discomfort, they had to **lie on** the cold ground during the camping trip.*

*She often preferred to **lie on** the beach and listen to the sound of the waves.*

Come on

To encourage or urge someone to do something; to express disbelief or impatience; to appear or make an appearance on television.

> *She playfully teased her friend, saying, "Don't be shy; **come on**, show us your dance moves!"*

> *He couldn't believe his luck and exclaimed, "Oh, **come on**! This is too good to be true!"*

> *It would be great if the expert could **come on** TV and provide insights into the current political situation.*

Count on

To rely on or trust someone or something; to depend on for support or assistance.

> *They knew they could always **count on** each other for help in times of need.*

> *Participants were encouraged to build strong relationships and be able to **count on** their teammates.*

> *He assured his team that they could **count on***

him to deliver high-quality work under tight deadlines.

*Despite the challenges, they continued to **count on** the support of their loyal customers.*

*She believed in the team's capabilities and told them, "You can **count on** us to succeed together."*

Bank on

To rely on or expect something to happen; to bet or depend on a particular outcome.

*They decided to **bank on** the success of the new marketing strategy to boost sales.*

*Participants were cautious not to **bank on** unrealistic projections and set achievable goals.*

*He knew it was risky to **bank on** a single client for the majority of their business.*

*Despite the uncertainties, they chose to **bank on** the experience and expertise of their team.*

*She advised her friend, "Don't **bank on** winning the lottery; focus on realistic financial planning."*

Go back on

To break a promise, commitment, or agreement; to fail to keep one's word.

> He regretted the decision to **go back on** his promise to attend the event and apologized to his friends.

> Participants discussed the consequences of choosing to **go back on** contractual agreements in business.

> She felt guilty when she had to **go back on** her commitment to volunteer due to unexpected circumstances.

> Despite initial assurances, they had to **go back on** the proposed timeline for the project due to unforeseen delays.

> He learned a valuable lesson about the importance of not **going back on** agreements to maintain trust in relationships.

Have on

To be wearing or dressed in a particular way; to possess or carry something.

*She decided to **have on** her favorite outfit for the special occasion.*

*Participants were advised to **have on** appropriate attire for the formal business meeting.*

*He realized he didn't **have on** his ID badge and had to go back to retrieve it.*

*Despite the warm weather, they chose to **have on** jackets for the outdoor activity to stay prepared.*

*She always made sure to **have on** comfortable shoes for the long walks during travel.*

Touch on

To briefly mention or discuss a topic; to bring up or allude to something briefly.

*During the presentation, he decided to **touch on** the key points to keep the audience engaged.*

*Participants were reminded to **touch on** important updates during the team meeting to keep everyone informed.*

*She chose to **touch on** the challenges faced by the*

team and discuss potential solutions.

*Despite time constraints, they managed to **touch on** the main aspects of the project during the client meeting.*

*He skillfully **touched on** the sensitive issue without dwelling on it for too long.*

Come up with

To think of or create something, such as an idea, plan, or solution.

*She managed to **come up with** a brilliant idea for the new marketing campaign.*

*Participants were encouraged to brainstorm and **come up with** innovative solutions to the challenge.*

*He needed to **come up with** a creative project proposal to present to the client.*

*Despite the tight deadline, they were able to **come up with** a well-thought-out plan for the project.*

*She asked her team to **come up with** suggestions for improving workplace productivity.*

Go through

To experience or undergo a process, situation, or set of conditions.

> They had to **go through** a rigorous interview process to secure the job.

> Participants were asked to share their experiences of challenges they've had to **go through** in their careers.

> He knew he had to **go through** the necessary training before starting the new position.

> Despite the obstacles, they were determined to **go through** the entire project without compromising on quality.

> She reflected on the personal growth she had **gone through** during challenging times.

Pick up

To lift or take something from a surface; to acquire or learn something.

*She decided to **pick up** the fallen books and organize them on the shelf.*

*Participants were encouraged to **pick up** new skills during the training program.*

*He wanted to **pick up** some fresh produce from the farmers' market on the way home.*

*Despite initial challenges, they were able to **pick up** the pace and complete the project on time.*

*She hoped to **pick up** conversational phrases in a new language while traveling abroad.*

Put off

To postpone or delay something; to decide to do it at a later time.

*She had to **put off** the meeting until next week due to unexpected circumstances.*

*Participants were informed that the event had to be **put off** due to unforeseen weather conditions.*

*He regretted having to **put off** the vacation because of work commitments.*

*Despite the excitement, they decided to **put off** the celebration until everyone could attend.*

*She realized she needed to **put off** making a decision until she had more information.*

Look up

To search for information in a reference source; to seek or find information online.

*She decided to **look up** the definition of the unfamiliar word in the dictionary.*

*Participants were encouraged to **look up** relevant articles to enhance their knowledge on the topic.*

*He used his smartphone to quickly **look up** the address of the restaurant.*

*Despite being a new city, they managed to **look up** local attractions and places of interest.*

*She advised her friend to **look up** reviews before purchasing a product online.*

Take off

To Remove or Unfasten; to become airborne; to experience sudden success or popularity; to take a break or a brief period of time away from work.

Take off your coat before sitting down.

*She had to **take off** her shoes before entering the house.*

*The plane was scheduled to **take off** at 3:00 PM for the international flight.*

*The new fashion trend started to **take off** among young adults.*

*Despite the challenges, their business began to **take off** after implementing a new marketing strategy.*

*He decided to **take off** a few days from work to relax and recharge.*

Put down

To place something on a surface; to criticize or belittle someone; to euthanize an animal; to record in writing.

*She decided to **put down** the heavy boxes before continuing with the task.*

*It's important not to **put down** others based on their differences.*

*They sadly had to make the decision to **put down** their elderly dog due to illness.*

*Despite the criticisms, he chose not to **put down** his colleagues but instead offered constructive feedback.*

*She grabbed a notebook to **put down** the important points discussed during the meeting.*

Put up with

To tolerate or endure someone or something unpleasant; to accept a difficult situation without complaining.

*She had to **put up with** noisy neighbors playing loud music late at night.*

*Participants were advised to address conflicts rather than **putting up with** a toxic work environment.*

*He realized he could no longer **put up with** the constant delays in the project.*

*Despite the challenges, they chose to **put up with** the inconveniences of living in a remote area.*

*She decided it was time to speak up and not **put up with** unfair treatment any longer.*

Make up

To create or invent something; to reconcile after a disagreement; to apply cosmetics.

*She decided to **make up** a story to explain her unexpected absence.*

*After the argument, they took some time to **make up** and rebuild their friendship.*

*He needed to **make up** his face before going on stage for the performance.*

*Despite the setbacks, they managed to **make up** for lost time and complete the project successfully.*

*She realized the importance of apologizing and trying to **make up** for the mistake.*

Turn down

To decrease the volume or intensity; to reject an offer
or request; to decline an invitation; to refuse.

> *She decided to **turn down** the music to avoid
> disturbing her neighbors.*
>
> *Despite the attractive job offer, he had to **turn
> down** the position due to personal reasons.*
>
> *They regretfully had to **turn down** the invitation
> to the event because of a prior commitment.*
>
> *Despite the pressure, she chose to **turn down** the
> business proposal as it didn't align with her
> values.*
>
> *He politely decided to **turn down** the offer to join
> the committee due to time constraints.*

Fall off

To decline in quantity, quality, or strength; to detach
or drop from a surface.

> *The number of attendees started to **fall off** as the
> event progressed.*

*Despite the initial excitement, interest in the product began to **fall off** over time.*

*He accidentally bumped the table, causing the items to **fall off** onto the floor.*

*Despite regular maintenance, the paint on the old building began to **fall off** in patches.*

*She noticed her performance at work starting to **fall off** due to increasing stress.*

Fall apart

To break into pieces; to disintegrate; to experience a sudden and complete failure or collapse.

*After years of wear and tear, the old book started to **fall apart**.*

*The relationship began to **fall apart** after a series of misunderstandings.*

*He tried to fix the antique chair, but it continued to **fall apart** with each use.*

*Despite their efforts, the team saw their plans **fall apart** due to unforeseen challenges.*

*She felt her world **fall apart** when she received the news of a significant personal loss.*

Wander off

To stray or deviate from a particular path or location without a specific purpose or intention.

*During the hike, they decided to **wander off** the main trail to explore the scenic surroundings.*

*Children should be supervised to ensure they don't **wander off** in crowded places.*

*He tends to **wander off** during conversations, lost in his own thoughts.*

*Despite the warning, the curious puppy managed to **wander off** from the backyard.*

*She realized she had unintentionally **wandered off** from the group during the nature walk.*

Sit out

To refrain from participating in an activity; to not take part in an event or situation.

*She decided to **sit out** the dance competition due to a minor injury.*

*Participants were given the option to **sit out** the team-building exercise if they preferred.*

*He chose to **sit out** the debate and observe the discussions from the sidelines.*

*Despite the invitation, they opted to **sit out** the family gathering to focus on personal priorities.*

*She recommended taking breaks to **sit out** of the intense work sessions for better productivity.*

Point out

To identify or draw attention to something; to highlight or indicate.

*She was quick to **point out** the errors in the report during the meeting.*

*Participants were encouraged to **point out** areas of improvement to enhance the project's quality.*

*He wanted to **point out** the significance of the historical landmarks during the tour.*

*Despite the complexity, they managed to **point out** the key features of the new software to the team.*

*She gently **pointed out** the importance of communication in building strong relationships.*

Blend in

To mix or merge with the surroundings; to fit in and be inconspicuous.

*She dressed casually to **blend in** with the crowd at the outdoor event.*

*Participants were advised to **blend in** with the local culture while traveling abroad.*

*He adjusted his approach to **blend in** seamlessly with the diverse team.*

*Despite being new to the neighborhood, they quickly managed to **blend in** with their friendly demeanor.*

*She learned to **blend in** with the corporate environment by adapting to the professional dress code.*

Jump ahead

To move forward quickly or advance to a later point in a sequence.

> She decided to **jump ahead** to the next chapter to see how the story unfolds.

> Despite the initial confusion, he managed to **jump ahead** in the queue at the airport.

> Participants were encouraged to think creatively and **jump ahead** to envision future possibilities.

> He couldn't resist the temptation to **jump ahead** and open one of the wrapped presents before the celebration.

> She suggested we **jump ahead** in the agenda to address the urgent matters first.

Put aside

To save or reserve something for later use; to set aside time or money for a specific purpose.

> She decided to **put aside** a portion of her salary for emergency expenses.

*Despite the busy schedule, he made a conscious effort to **put aside** time for self-care activities.*

*Participants were advised to **put aside** personal differences and focus on the common goal.*

*He suggested they **put aside** some funds for a future vacation or special occasion.*

*She realized the importance of learning to **put aside** negative thoughts for a more positive mindset.*

Set aside

To reserve or allocate something for a specific purpose; to consciously disregard or ignore personal biases.

*She decided to **set aside** a quiet corner in the room for focused study sessions.*

*Despite the distractions, he managed to **set aside** dedicated time for daily meditation.*

*He urged the team to **set aside** a budget for research and development initiatives.*

*She recommended they **set aside** a specific area in the garden for growing vegetables.*

*To reach a fair verdict, jurors must **set aside** any preconceived notions about the defendant.*

*Participants were instructed to **set aside** personal biases and approach the problem objectively.*

Turn up

To appear or arrive; to increase in volume or intensity; to happen unexpectedly.

*She promised to **turn up** for the meeting despite her busy schedule.*

*Despite the initial low turnout, more participants started to **turn up** as the event progressed.*

*He decided to **turn up** the music to create a lively atmosphere at the party.*

*Despite the careful planning, unexpected challenges can **turn up** during project implementation.*

*She hoped that a solution would **turn up** as they*

explored different options.

Get away with

To escape punishment or consequences for something; to succeed in doing something without being caught or detected.

*She couldn't believe she managed to **get away with** arriving late to the meeting.*

*Despite the suspicions, he somehow always found a way to **get away with** breaking the rules.*

*Participants were reminded that it's not ethical to attempt to **get away with** plagiarism in academic settings.*

*He realized he couldn't **get away with** skipping his responsibilities without facing consequences.*

*She hoped the thief wouldn't **get away with** stealing her belongings, and justice would be served.*

Take in

To absorb information; to bring something or

someone into a particular space or place.

> *She needed a moment to **take in** the breathtaking view from the mountaintop.*

> *Despite the complexity, he managed to **take in** the details of the intricate painting.*

> *Participants were encouraged to actively listen and **take in** the valuable insights shared during the seminar.*

> *He decided to **take in** a stray cat and provide it with a loving home.*

> *She asked him to **take in** the measurements for the custom-made furniture.*

Take over

To assume control or responsibility; to become the dominant influence or force.

> *She had to **take over** the project when the team lead fell ill.*

> *Despite initial challenges, he successfully managed to **take over** the management of the company.*

*Participants were instructed to collaborate and seamlessly **take over** tasks during the transition period.*

*He realized it was time to **take over** the family business after his father's retirement.*

*She was determined to **take over** as the team captain and lead the group to victory.*

Bring up

To mention or introduce a topic into conversation; to raise or nurture a child.

*She decided to **bring up** the issue during the team meeting for discussion.*

*Despite the discomfort, he chose to **bring up** the sensitive matter with his friend.*

*Participants were encouraged to **bring up** any concerns or suggestions for improvement.*

*He promised himself to **bring up** the idea of flexible working hours with the management.*

*She and her partner decided to **bring up** their*

children in a multicultural environment.

Take out on

To express frustration, anger, or negative emotions towards someone or something unrelated to the cause of those emotions.

> *She apologized for **taking out her frustration on** her colleagues during a stressful period.*

> *Despite the difficult day, he refrained from **taking out his anger on** his family.*

> *Participants were reminded not to **take out their stress on** their teammates.*

> *He regretted **taking out his irritation on** a coworker and later apologized.*

Fill in

To provide information or details; to complete or substitute for someone or something temporarily.

> *She was asked to **fill in** the missing details in the report before the deadline.*

*Despite the absence, he managed to **fill in** for his colleague during their vacation.*

*Participants were given a form to **fill in** with their contact information.*

*He agreed to **fill in** as the team leader until a permanent replacement was found.*

*She volunteered to **fill in** for the receptionist during her lunch break.*

Put on

To wear clothing or accessories; to apply makeup or perfume; to organize or stage an event.

*She decided to **put on** her favorite dress for the special occasion.*

*Despite the casual setting, he chose to **put on** a suit to make a good impression.*

*Participants were advised to **put on** comfortable attire for the team-building exercise.*

*He asked her to help him **put on** the costume for the school play.*

*She volunteered to **put on** a fundraising event for the local charity.*

Fake out

To deceive or trick someone by making them believe something false or misleading.

*He tried to **fake out** the opponent by pretending to go in one direction and then quickly changing course.*

*Despite the disguise, she couldn't **fake out** her friends, who recognized her immediately.*

*Participants were challenged to use clever tactics to **fake out** their opponents in the strategic game.*

*He managed to **fake out** the security system and gain unauthorized access.*

*She used misdirection to **fake out** the audience during her magic performance.*

Run out of

To exhaust the supply or availability of something; to

deplete the quantity of a resource.

> *They realized they were about to **run out of** fuel and needed to find a gas station quickly.*

> *Despite the careful planning, they unexpectedly **ran out of** snacks during the road trip.*

> *Participants were warned not to **run out of** water during the hiking expedition in the desert.*

> *He had to pause the production as they **ran out of** raw materials for the manufacturing process.*

> *She made a grocery list to ensure she wouldn't **run out of** essential items for the week.*

Take back

To retract or withdraw a statement, offer, or invitation; to return something to its original place.

> *Realizing the mistake, he decided to **take back** his earlier criticism of the project.*

> *Despite the initial refusal, they later agreed to **take back** the job offer.*

> *Participants were encouraged to **take back** any

offensive remarks and maintain a positive discussion environment.

*She had to **take back** the borrowed book to return it to the library on time.*

*He apologized and offered to **take back** the hurtful words he had said in the heat of the moment.*

Work out

To exercise or engage in physical activity; to solve a problem or reach a successful conclusion.

*She decided to **work out** at the gym for an hour to stay fit and healthy.*

*Despite the initial challenges, they managed to **work out** a compromise that satisfied both parties.*

*Participants were advised to **work out** regularly to maintain a balanced and active lifestyle.*

*He needed some time to **work out** the complex math problem before providing an answer.*

She believed that with dedication and

*perseverance, any issue could be **worked out**.*

Come across

To encounter or find unexpectedly; to make a particular impression or be perceived in a certain way.

*During their hike, they **came across** a hidden waterfall in the dense forest.*

*Despite the vast library, she unexpectedly **came across** the book she had been searching for.*

*Participants were asked to share personal experiences where they **came across** challenges and overcame them.*

*He often **comes across** as confident in professional settings, which enhances his leadership image.*

*She didn't expect to **come across** old photos that brought back fond memories while cleaning the attic.*

Look after

To take care of or be responsible for someone or something.

> She promised to **look after** her neighbor's plants while they were on vacation.

> Despite the busy schedule, he always finds time to **look after** his younger siblings.

> Participants were reminded to **look after** their well-being and prioritize self-care.

> He agreed to **look after** the office in the absence of the manager.

> She volunteered to **look after** the stray kittens until they found permanent homes.

Put together

To assemble or create something by combining various elements.

> They collaborated to **put together** an impressive presentation for the client.

> Despite the limited resources, he managed to **put together** a makeshift shelter in the wilderness.

*Participants were instructed to **put together** a team and brainstorm innovative ideas for the project.*

*He decided to **put together** a puzzle with his family during the rainy weekend.*

*She and her friends worked hard to **put together** a surprise birthday party for their colleague.*

Put through

To connect someone by phone; to complete a process or procedure.

*She asked the receptionist to **put her through** to the manager's office.*

*Despite the technical issues, he managed to **put through** the urgent order for shipment.*

*Participants were advised to use the automated system to **put through** their requests efficiently.*

*He requested the operator to **put him through** to the customer service department.*

*She patiently waited for the assistant to **put***

__through__ the call to the conference room.

Hold on

To wait or pause; to grasp or cling to something.

She asked the team to __hold on__ for a moment while she fetched the necessary documents.

Despite the uncertainty, he encouraged everyone to __hold on__ and remain optimistic about the future.

Participants were requested to __hold on__ to their tickets until the rescheduled event date was confirmed.

He needed to __hold on__ to the railing while climbing the steep stairs.

She told her friend to __hold on__ to the gift until she returned from her trip.

Look into

To investigate or examine; to explore a matter or situation.

*They decided to **look into** the recent increase in customer complaints to identify the root cause.*

*Despite the initial confusion, he promised to **look into** the billing discrepancy and resolve it promptly.*

*Participants were encouraged to **look into** new technologies to enhance their productivity.*

*He assured the team that he would **look into** the feasibility of the proposed project.*

*She suggested they **look into** alternative solutions before making a final decision.*

Come back

To return to a place; to recover from a setback or disappointment.

*She promised to **come back** to the office after the meeting concluded.*

*Despite the challenges, he was determined to **come back** stronger and more resilient.*

Participants were encouraged to take breaks and

*refresh their minds, ready to **come back** with renewed focus.*

*He assured his teammates that he would **come back** after a short break to continue working on the project.*

Call on

To visit or pay a visit to someone; to request or demand.

*She decided to **call on** her friend to check how they were doing after the illness.*

*Despite the busy schedule, he made time to **call on** his grandparents over the weekend.*

*During the crisis, the community **called on** local businesses for support.*

*The president **called on** the nations to unite in the face of the global challenge.*

Carry on

To continue or proceed with an activity; to persist in doing something.

*Despite the setback, they decided to **carry on** with the project and find alternative solutions.*

*He urged the team to **carry on** with the task at hand and not be discouraged by minor obstacles.*

*Participants were advised to **carry on** with their regular work while the technical issue was being resolved.*

*She chose to **carry on** with her studies despite facing challenges along the way.*

*He encouraged his friend to **carry on** with the exercise routine for better health.*

Come up

To arise or happen; to present itself; to approach someone for a conversation or request; to devise or think of.

*She couldn't attend the meeting as something unexpected **came up** at the last minute.*

*Despite the challenges, a new opportunity **came up** for them to showcase their skills.*

*Participants were encouraged to share any ideas that **came up** during the brainstorming session.*

*He waited for the right moment to **come up** and discuss his concerns with the manager.*

*She decided to **come up** with a creative solution to the problem that had been bothering her for days.*

Work on

To focus effort and attention on a task or project; to make progress in developing or improving something.

*She dedicated time every day to **work on** improving her language skills.*

*Despite the distractions, he managed to **work on** the report and meet the deadline.*

*Participants were advised to **work on** their communication skills to enhance collaboration within the team.*

*He decided to **work on** building a strong foundation for his startup before expanding.*

Slack off

To work less diligently or with less effort than usual; to be lazy or neglectful of responsibilities.

*Despite the approaching deadline, he chose to **slack off** and procrastinate.*

*She received a warning from her supervisor for consistently **slacking off** during work hours.*

*Participants were reminded not to **slack off** in adhering to safety protocols in the workplace.*

*He acknowledged his mistake and promised not to **slack off** in completing his assignments on time.*

*She realized the importance of not **slacking off** in her studies if she wanted to achieve her goals.*

Drop off

To deliver or leave someone or something at a
destination; to decrease in amount or intensity.

> *She asked him to **drop off** the package at the
> post office on his way home.*

> *Despite the traffic, they managed to **drop off** the
> kids at school on time.*

> *Participants were instructed to **drop off** their
> completed forms at the registration desk.*

> *He decided to **drop off** the donation at the
> charity organization to support their cause.*

> *She offered to **drop off** the groceries at her
> neighbor's doorstep as a gesture of kindness.*

Come out

To be released or become available; to reveal or
disclose information; to attend a social event.

> *The new book by the author is set to **come out**
> next month.*

> *Despite the secrecy, the truth eventually **came
> out** during the investigation.*

*Participants were excited about the upcoming product launch and couldn't wait for details to **come out**.*

*He decided to **come out** about his feelings and share them with his close friends.*

*She was thrilled to **come out** to the party and celebrate with her friends.*

Look out

To be watchful or vigilant; to be cautious or aware of potential dangers.

*She warned the children to **look out** for cars before crossing the street.*

*Despite the clear path, they were advised to **look out** for obstacles during the hike.*

*Participants were reminded to **look out** for signs of fatigue and take breaks during the long journey.*

*He instructed his team to **look out** for any suspicious activity in the neighborhood.*

She used binoculars to **look out** for rare birds during the bird-watching expedition.

Turn off

To switch off or shut down; to lose interest or be unappealing; to divert from a path.

She asked him to **turn off** the lights before leaving the room.

Despite the engaging storyline, some viewers chose to **turn off** the movie halfway through.

Participants were advised to **turn off** electronic devices during the meditation session.

He decided to **turn off** the TV and spend quality time with his family.

She encouraged her friend to **turn off** negative thoughts and focus on positive aspects of life.

Take away

To remove, subtract, or eliminate something; to provide food for consumption outside the establishment; to derive or gain.

*If you **take away** 10 from 15, you're left with 5.*

*He decided to **take away** the old furniture to make room for the new ones.*

*Can you please **take away** the empty dishes from the table?*

*Participants were given the option to **take away** lunch and enjoy it in the park.*

*She chose to **take away** the negativity and focus on the positive aspects of the situation.*

*Despite the challenges, they managed to **take away** valuable lessons from the experience.*

Make out

To perceive or understand something; to engage in kissing and other intimate activities; to achieve or complete something, often with effort; to pretend or claim falsely; to write or complete a document, such as a check or form.

*She couldn't **make out** the details of the distant object without her glasses.*

*She and her partner chose to **make out** on the beach while enjoying the sunset.*

*She worked hard to **make out** a successful career.*

*He tried to **make out** that he was innocent.*

*He had to **make out** a check for the rent.*

Look up to

To admire or respect someone; to regard someone as a role model.

*She always **looked up to** her older sister as a source of guidance and inspiration.*

*Despite the challenges, he managed to **look up to** his mentor for valuable advice and support.*

*Participants were encouraged to **look up to** leaders who exhibited qualities of integrity and compassion.*

*He decided to **look up to** historical figures who had overcome adversity for motivation.*

*She realized that her students **looked up to** her*

as a role model, and she embraced the responsibility.

Turn in

To submit or hand over something; to go to bed or retire for the night.

*She was required to **turn in** her completed assignment by the end of the day.*

*Despite the late hour, he decided to **turn in** and get a good night's sleep.*

*Participants were instructed to **turn in** their feedback forms before leaving the event.*

*He promised to **turn in** the project report by the deadline set by the client.*

*She realized it was time to **turn in** after a long and exhausting day at work.*

Hand in

To submit or deliver something, especially a written assignment or document.

*She asked the students to **hand in** their essays by the end of the class.*

*Despite the tight deadline, he managed to **hand in** the project proposal on time.*

*Participants were reminded to **hand in** their registration forms at the reception desk.*

*He decided to **hand in** his resignation letter and explore new opportunities.*

*She urged her team to **hand in** their progress reports for the quarterly review.*

Pass out

To distribute something; to lose consciousness briefly.

*She decided to **pass out** flyers to promote the upcoming event.*

*Despite the heat, he cautioned participants not to **pass out** during the outdoor activity.*

*Participants were excited to **pass out** promotional items to attract visitors to their booth.*

*He realized he needed to take a break before he would **pass out** from exhaustion.*

*She suggested having a first aid kit on hand in case anyone were to **pass out** during the intense workout session.*

Run into

To encounter or meet unexpectedly; to collide with or bump into something.

*She was surprised to **run into** her childhood friend at the grocery store.*

*Despite the busy city, he managed to **run into** a colleague while grabbing coffee.*

*Participants were encouraged to network and potentially **run into** professionals from their industry.*

*He apologized after accidentally **running into** a pedestrian while riding his bike.*

*She suggested being cautious while driving to avoid **running into** unexpected obstacles on the road.*

Put up

To display or exhibit; to tolerate or endure; to provide accommodations or host someone.

> *She decided to **put up** a poster to announce the upcoming event.*

> *Despite the challenging situation, he managed to **put up** a brave front and stay positive.*

> *Participants were asked to **put up** with temporary inconveniences during the construction phase.*

> *He offered to **put up** his friends who were visiting from out of town.*

> *She suggested using a tent to **put up** shelter during the camping trip.*

Carry out

To complete or fulfill a task, plan, or action; to conduct or perform an activity.

> *The team was able to **carry out** the project successfully within the given timeframe.*

> *Despite the challenges, they managed to **carry***

out the experiment and gather valuable data.

*Participants were instructed to **carry out** the assigned tasks and report their findings.*

*He decided to **carry out** a survey to gather feedback from customers about the product.*

*She was determined to **carry out** her plan to organize a community event for charity.*

Grow into

To mature or develop into a particular state, role, or size over time.

*The small sapling eventually **grew into** a towering oak tree.*

*The shy child gradually **grew into** a confident and outgoing individual.*

*Starting as an intern, he **grew into** a skilled and experienced professional in the company.*

*She realized that her passion for art was starting to **grow into** a potential career path.*

*He witnessed the business **grow into** a successful*

enterprise over the years.

*When my daughter was younger, we bought her clothes a size larger, knowing she would eventually grow **into** them.*

Grow out

To let something, typically hair or plants, become longer or larger over time.

*She decided to **grow out** her hair and embrace a new look.*

*Despite the initial awkward phase, he chose to **grow out** his beard for a change.*

*Participants were asked if they wanted to **grow out** their plants for a more natural landscape.*

*He decided to **grow out** his garden and experiment with different types of plants.*

*She realized that allowing her hair to **grow out** was a liberating and empowering choice.*

Drop out

To leave or withdraw from a course, program, or activity, typically before completion.

> *Despite the initial enthusiasm, he decided to **drop out** of the university due to personal reasons.*

> *She realized that the chosen field of study was not her passion and chose to **drop out**.*

> *Participants were reminded of the importance of seeking support if they were considering **dropping out** of the program.*

> *He faced challenges but was determined not to **drop out** and persevered to complete his degree.*

> *She explained her decision to **drop out** of the competition and focus on other priorities.*

Flunk out

To fail academically and be required to leave an educational institution.

> *Despite the effort, he was unable to keep up with the coursework and eventually **flunked out** of college.*

> *She faced challenges in adjusting to the academic*

*workload and eventually **flunked out** of the program.*

*Participants were warned about the consequences of consistent poor performance leading to **flunking out**.*

*He sought help from tutors to avoid **flunking out** and successfully improved his grades.*

*She reflected on the reasons that led her to **flunk out** and decided to take a different approach to her studies.*

Turn out

To result or develop in a particular way; to attend or appear at an event.

*Despite initial doubts, the project **turned out** to be a great success.*

*He wondered how the experiment would **turn out** and eagerly awaited the results.*

*Many citizens **turned out** to express their concerns at the environmental rally.*

*Despite the rain, a large crowd **turned out** for the*

outdoor concert.

Fall back on

To rely on or resort to something as a backup or alternative when facing difficulties or challenges.

*When the original plan failed, they had to **fall back on** their contingency strategy.*

*Despite the setbacks, she knew she could **fall back on** her supportive friends for help.*

*Participants were advised to have a backup plan they could **fall back on** in case of unexpected changes.*

*He decided to **fall back on** his savings to cover unexpected expenses.*

*She realized she could **fall back on** her problem-solving skills when facing challenges at work.*

Fall behind

To lag or be slower in progress compared to others; to be unable to keep up with a schedule or pace.

*Despite the effort, he started to **fall behind** in completing the assigned tasks.*

*She faced challenges that caused her to **fall behind** in the race.*

*Participants were warned about the consequences of consistently **falling behind** in their coursework.*

*He struggled not to **fall behind** in the competitive industry by staying updated on industry trends.*

*She sought additional support to avoid **falling behind** in meeting project deadlines.*

Look around

To explore or examine the surrounding environment; to search for something.

*She decided to **look around** the new neighborhood to familiarize herself with the surroundings.*

*Despite the crowded market, he managed to **look around** for unique souvenirs.*

*Participants were encouraged to **look around** and discover hidden gems in the city.*

*He asked the team to **look around** the office for any misplaced documents.*

*She decided to **look around** online for reviews before making a purchase decision.*

Pull off

To successfully accomplish or achieve something, often despite challenges or difficulty.

*Despite the complexity, they managed to **pull off** the event without any major issues.*

*She was thrilled to successfully **pull off** the challenging dance routine.*

*Participants worked together to **pull off** a successful fundraising campaign for the charity.*

*He needed the entire team's effort to **pull off** the ambitious project ahead of schedule.*

*She demonstrated creativity and determination to **pull off** an impressive art exhibition.*

Come to

To regain consciousness; to reach a particular result or understanding.

*After the accident, it took him a moment to **come to** and assess the situation.*

*She needed time to **come to** terms with the unexpected news.*

*Participants were asked to **come to** a consensus on the best approach for the project.*

*He hoped that the team would eventually **come to** an agreement on the decision.*

*She urged everyone to **come to** the meeting with open minds and a willingness to collaborate.*

Make do with

To manage or cope with the resources or circumstances available, even if they are not ideal.

*Despite the limited ingredients, she managed to **make do with** what was available and create a delicious meal.*

*He decided to **make do with** the outdated equipment until new ones arrived.*

*Participants were challenged to **make do with** a smaller budget for their creative projects.*

*She had to **make do with** a temporary workspace while the office underwent renovations.*

*He encouraged the team to be innovative and find ways to **make do with** the existing resources.*

Hang up

To end a phone call; to suspend or place something on a hook or hanger.

*I'm going to **hang up** now. I'll talk to you later.*

*She **hung up** on me before I could even finish my sentence!*

*Can you please **hang up** your coat in the closet?*

*After washing, I always **hang up** my wet towels to dry*

Pounce on

To attack or seize quickly and aggressively; to take advantage of an opportunity promptly.

> *The cat waited patiently to **pounce on** the unsuspecting mouse in the backyard.*

> *Despite the surprise, he managed to **pounce on** the chance to showcase his talent.*

> *Participants were encouraged to be proactive and **pounce on** opportunities for collaboration.*

> *He decided to **pounce on** the moment and propose a creative solution to the problem.*

> *She urged the team to **pounce on** market trends and stay ahead of the competition.*

Join in

To participate or become involved in an activity or group; to join others in doing something.

> *She was excited to **join in** the dance performance and showcase her skills.*

> *Despite the initial hesitation, he decided to **join in***

the team-building exercise.

*Participants were invited to **join in** the discussion and share their perspectives.*

*He encouraged everyone to **join in** the charity event and contribute to the cause.*

*She decided to **join in** the celebration and share the joy with her friends.*

Result in

To lead to or cause a particular outcome or consequence.

*The team's hard work and dedication **resulted in** a successful product launch.*

*Despite the challenges, their collaborative efforts **resulted in** a positive impact on the community.*

*Participants were optimistic that their innovative ideas would **result in** positive changes in the organization.*

*He believed that consistent effort and perseverance would **result in** achieving his long-term goals.*

*She hoped that the negotiations would **result in** a mutually beneficial agreement for both parties.*

Succeed in

To achieve a goal or desired outcome; to accomplish or prosper in a particular endeavor.

*Despite the initial challenges, she managed to **succeed in** completing the project ahead of schedule.*

*He was determined to **succeed in** his career and worked hard to achieve his aspirations.*

*Participants were inspired to set ambitious goals and work tirelessly to **succeed in** their chosen fields.*

*She believed that a positive mindset and perseverance were key to **succeeding in** any endeavor.*

*He acknowledged the team's efforts and emphasized the importance of collaboration to **succeed in** their collective goals.*

Engage in

To participate or become involved in a particular activity, often willingly or actively.

*She decided to **engage in** volunteer work to contribute to the community.*

*Despite the busy schedule, he found time to **engage in** a hobby that brought him joy.*

*Participants were encouraged to **engage in** open dialogue and share their perspectives.*

*He believed it was essential to **engage in** continuous learning to stay updated in his field.*

*She urged the team to **engage in** team-building activities to strengthen collaboration.*

Cave in

To collapse or give way, especially under pressure or force; to submit or surrender under pressure.

*The old building's roof started to sag and eventually **caved in** after heavy rainfall.*

Despite the resistance, the opposition eventually

caved in to the demands of the negotiation team.

Participants were cautioned about the potential risks of structures that could **cave in** *due to structural weaknesses.*

He emphasized the importance of resilience and not allowing one's principles to **cave in** *under external pressure.*

She urged the team to stay united and not **cave in** *to external pressures that could compromise their values.*

Bring in

To introduce or bring something or someone to a particular place; to involve or include in a situation.

The company decided to **bring in** *a consultant to provide expertise on the new project.*

Despite initial hesitations, they chose to **bring in** *a new team member to enhance diversity and skills.*

Participants were excited to hear about the plans to **bring in** *cutting-edge technology to improve efficiency.*

*He suggested the need to **bring in** additional resources to meet the growing demands of the project.*

*She decided to **bring in** external perspectives by inviting guest speakers to the conference.*

Fall in

To collapse or descend; to form a line or queue; to agree or conform; to participate or join; to begin associating with.

*The old building began to deteriorate, and eventually, a section of the roof **fell in**.*

*Due to heavy rainfall, the riverbank started to erode, causing part of it to **fall in**.*

*As the students gathered in the courtyard, they were instructed to **fall in** before marching.*

*Before the parade, the soldiers were ordered to **fall in** and get into formation.*

*After much discussion, the committee members agreed to **fall in with** the majority opinion.*

*Several volunteers decided to **fall in** and help with the community clean-up.*

*After starting college, he **fell in with** a group of students who were known for their rebellious behavior.*

Unit 7

Zero in on

To focus or direct attention on something specific; to target or pinpoint.

*The detective decided to **zero in on** a key witness to gather more information about the crime.*

*Despite the vast data, they managed to **zero in on** the critical factors influencing the project's success.*

*Participants were encouraged to **zero in on** the most relevant aspects of the discussion to save time.*

*He suggested using analytics tools to **zero in on** customer preferences and tailor marketing* *strategies.*

*She decided to **zero in on** specific skills during the training program to enhance individual strengths.*

Check in

To register one's arrival at a hotel, airport, or event; to inquire or confirm one's attendance or presence.

*Upon reaching the hotel, they proceeded to **check in** at the front desk to get their room keys.*

*Despite the busy schedule, he managed to **check in** at the conference venue on time.*

*Participants were reminded to **check in** using the provided app to streamline the event registration process.*

*He decided to **check in** early for the flight to secure a good seat.*

*She urged everyone to **check in** on the online platform to confirm their attendance at the virtual meeting.*

Check out

To complete the necessary formalities when leaving a hotel; To verify, inspect, or examine something; to pay for goods or services before leaving.

*We'll **check out** of the hotel tomorrow morning.*

*He suggested taking the time to **check out** the local attractions before leaving the city.*

*Could you **check out** that noise? I think something might be wrong with the engine.*

*Let's **check out** this new restaurant everyone is talking about.*

*After shopping, you can **check out** at the cashier.*

Check on

To inquire about someone or something; to verify or monitor a situation.

*She decided to **check on** her elderly neighbor to make sure he was okay during the storm.*

*Before leaving, he asked his friend to **check on** his pets while he was away.*

*The manager promised to **check on** the progress of the project regularly to ensure it stayed on track.*

*Parents often **check on** their sleeping children before going to bed themselves.*

*During the road trip, they would periodically **check on** the map to confirm their route.*

Log in

To enter one's credentials to access a computer system, website, or application.

*Users need to **log in** with their usernames and passwords to access the secure portal.*

*After signing up, you can **log in** to your account to manage your preferences.*

*Employees are required to **log in** at the beginning of their workday to access company systems.*

*Make sure to **log in** before attempting to make any changes to your account settings.*

*Students are encouraged to **log in** to the online*

platform for course materials and announcements.

Log out

To exit or sign out of a computer system, website, or application.

*It's important to **log out** of your email account when using a public computer.*

*After completing your work, don't forget to **log out** to ensure the security of your account.*

*Users are automatically **logged out** after a period of inactivity to protect their privacy.*

*Always remember to **log out** when using shared devices to prevent unauthorized access.*

*Before closing the browser, make sure to **log out** of any online accounts you may have accessed.*

Get on with

To continue or proceed with something; to have a harmonious relationship with someone.

*Despite the challenges, they decided to **get on with** the project and meet the deadline.*

*After the disagreement, they chose to **get on with** their respective tasks without dwelling on the conflict.*

*It's essential to **get on with** your colleagues to create a positive work environment.*

*Instead of dwelling on the past, they agreed to **get on with** their lives and focus on the future.*

*Let's put the differences aside and **get on with** the task at hand.*

Settle on

To decide on or choose after consideration; to reach a conclusion or agreement.

*After much discussion, they finally **settled on** a date for the meeting.*

*It took a while, but they eventually **settled on** a design for the new website.*

*When house hunting, it's important to **settle on***

the features that matter most to you.

*After exploring various options, they were able to **settle on** a restaurant that everyone agreed on.*

*It's time to **settle on** a decision and move forward with the plan.*

Seize on

To take advantage of an opportunity quickly and decisively; to grasp or grab onto.

*Entrepreneurs often need to **seize on** emerging trends to stay ahead in the market.*

*She was quick to **seize on** the chance to showcase her talent when the opportunity arose.*

*Investors who can **seize on** timely opportunities may experience significant returns.*

*During negotiations, it's crucial to **seize on** any favorable terms that may arise.*

*When a great idea comes along, it's important to **seize on** it before someone else does.*

Bring on

To cause or initiate something, often enthusiastically;
to invite or welcome.

> *With the new project underway, they were excited
> to **bring on** fresh ideas and perspectives.*

> *As the celebration approached, they decided to
> **bring on** additional entertainment for the guests.*

> *He wanted to **bring on** a positive change in the
> team by introducing innovative strategies.*

> *The coach encouraged the players to **bring on**
> their best performance for the upcoming match.*

> *Despite the challenges, they were ready to **bring
> on** the next phase of the project.*

Focus on

To concentrate attention or effort on a specific task or
goal; to direct one's attention towards.

> *It's important to **focus on** the key aspects of the
> project to ensure its success.*

> *Before the exam, she decided to **focus on***

studying the most challenging topics.

*Amidst distractions, he managed to **focus on** completing the critical tasks for the day.*

*Leaders often need to **focus on** the long-term vision while navigating daily challenges.*

*Teams should **focus on** collaboration to achieve common objectives.*

Insist on

To demand or assert firmly; to maintain a position or opinion with determination.

*She would always **insist on** using high-quality materials for her artwork.*

*Despite the challenges, he continued to **insist on** implementing ethical practices in the business.*

*Parents often **insist on** certain rules to ensure the well-being of their children.*

*The coach would **insist on** discipline and hard work from the players to achieve success.*

During negotiations, it's common for each party

*to **insist on** specific terms.*

Catch on

To understand or grasp a concept; to become popular or widely accepted.

*After some explanation, she finally began to **catch on** to the new software.*

*The innovative idea quickly began to **catch on** in the industry.*

*Students who actively participate in class tend to **catch on** to new concepts more quickly.*

*As the benefits became evident, the community started to **catch on** to the importance of recycling.*

*It took a while for the new trend to **catch on** among consumers.*

Clock off

To record the end of one's work shift by noting the time on a time clock; to finish work.

Clock out

To officially record the end of one's work hours; to finish working and leave the workplace.

__clock out__ and enjoy her evening.

It's essential to remember to __clock out__ even if leaving the workplace briefly.

Employees should ensure they __clock out__ properly to avoid any discrepancies in their attendance records.

Punch in

To record the beginning of one's work hours, often by using a time clock; to officially start the workday.

Employees are required to __punch in__ at the beginning of their scheduled shift.

Before starting their tasks, workers need to __punch in__ to officially begin the workday.

The system automatically records the time when employees __punch in__ at the start of the day.

It's crucial to remember to __punch in__ upon arriving at the workplace to accurately track working hours.

Employees should __punch in__ promptly to ensure proper attendance records and payment for their work.

Punch out

To record the end of one's work hours, often by using a time clock; to officially leave the workplace.

*Employees are required to **punch out** at the end of their scheduled shift.*

*Before leaving for the day, make sure to **punch out** to accurately track working hours.*

*After completing the final task, he was ready to **punch out** and head home.*

*It's crucial to remember to **punch out** even if leaving the workplace for a short break.*

*The system automatically records the time when employees **punch out** at the end of the day.*

Dash off

To leave or depart hastily; to write or create something quickly.

*As soon as the meeting concluded, he had to **dash***

off to catch his flight.

*Feeling inspired, she decided to **dash off** a quick poem in her notebook.*

*Before the event, he needed to **dash off** a few emails to finalize the arrangements.*

*She had to **dash off** to make it to the appointment on time.*

*In a hurry, they had to **dash off** without saying proper goodbyes.*

Doze off

To fall asleep, especially unintentionally or briefly.

*After a long day at work, he often found himself starting to **doze off** on the couch.*

*During the boring lecture, some students tend to **doze off** without even realizing it.*

*She decided to take a short break and unintentionally **dozed off** at her desk.*

*As the soothing music played, he began to **doze off** in the comfortable chair.*

*Despite trying to stay awake, exhaustion took over, and she started to **doze off** during the movie.*

Ease off

To gradually reduce in intensity or pressure; to become less strict or demanding.

*After the hectic period, the workload began to **ease off**, allowing for a more relaxed pace.*

*As the storm passed, the wind started to **ease off**, and the weather improved.*

*The manager decided to **ease off** on the strict policies to boost employee morale.*

*He asked the chef to **ease off** on the spice in the dish, as some customers found it too hot.*

*As tensions decreased, the company began to **ease off** on certain restrictions for the employees.*

Get off

To disembark from a vehicle or mode of transportation; to leave a place or situation.

> *Passengers are requested to **get off** the bus only at designated stops.*

> *After the long flight, they were eager to **get off** the plane and stretch their legs.*

> *It's time to **get off** the train; our destination is the next station.*

> *Despite the rain, they decided to **get off** and explore the charming town.*

> *After the meeting, employees were relieved to **get off** and enjoy their lunch break.*

Head off

To depart or leave for a destination; to take action to prevent a situation or problem.

> *Before the traffic gets heavy, let's **head off** for the airport.*

> *She decided to **head off** early to avoid the rush-hour traffic.*

*The team planned to **head off** potential issues by addressing them in the initial stages of the project.*

*He had to **head off** a conflict by mediating between the two parties.*

*By addressing the concerns early, they were able to **head off** any major setbacks in the project.*

Log off

To sign out or disconnect from a computer system, website, or application.

*Before leaving the office, make sure to **log off** your computer to secure your data.*

*Users are encouraged to **log off** from their accounts when using public computers.*

*After completing your tasks, it's essential to **log off** to protect your privacy.*

*Employees were reminded to **log off** from shared devices to prevent unauthorized access.*

*Always remember to **log off** when using online*

platforms on shared computers.

Reel off

To recite or say something quickly and effortlessly; to list or narrate in a rapid manner.

*During the interview, he was able to **reel off** the accomplishments of the team without hesitation.*

*She can **reel off** the names of all the capitals in alphabetical order.*

*As the teacher asked questions, the student continued to **reel off** the answers with confidence.*

*When prompted, he could **reel off** the details of the project effortlessly.*

*As an expert in the field, she could easily **reel off** facts and statistics during presentations.*

Tell off

To scold or reprimand someone strongly; to express disapproval or anger.

*She had to **tell off** her colleague for consistently*

arriving late to meetings.

*After the mistake, the manager decided to **tell off** the team responsible for the error.*

*Parents sometimes need to **tell off** their children to correct their behavior.*

*The teacher didn't hesitate to **tell off** the students for not completing their assignments on time.*

*Despite being friends, he felt it was necessary to **tell off** his friend for breaking a promise.*

Wear off

To diminish or fade over time; to lose effectiveness or intensity.

*After a while, the excitement of the new job began to **wear off**.*

*The effects of the pain reliever will **wear off** gradually, so take it as directed.*

*The novelty of the gadget quickly **wore off** after a few weeks of use.*

Over time, the initial charm of the relationship

*can **wear off**, requiring effort to maintain.*

Wipe off

To remove or clean something by rubbing or using a cloth; to erase or eliminate.

*She needed to **wipe off** the dust from the old books on the shelf.*

*After the spill, he quickly grabbed a towel to **wipe off** the coffee from the table.*

*Before serving, make sure to **wipe off** any residue from the kitchen counter.*

*The whiteboard was filled with notes, and they decided to **wipe off** the information to start fresh.*

*Use a damp cloth to **wipe off** the dirt and grime from the surface of the furniture.*

Write off

To consider something as a loss or failure; to acknowledge that it has no value or chance of success.

*After numerous attempts to repair the old car, they decided to **write off** the vehicle as beyond repair.*

*Due to financial challenges, the company had to **write off** some of its outstanding debts.*

*Despite the initial investment, they had to **write off** the failed project as a learning experience.*

*It's essential to know when to **write off** a business idea that is not gaining traction in the market.*

*After careful assessment, the accountant recommended to **write off** the obsolete inventory.*

Block off

To obstruct or close a passage or area.

*The construction crew had to **block off** the road for repairs, causing a temporary detour for drivers.*

*They decided to **block off** a section of the park for a private event.*

During the event, security personnel were

Break off

To separate or detach from something; to stop or discontinue a relationship, conversation, or activity.

*He had to **break off** a piece of the chocolate bar to share with his friends.*

*Due to irreconcilable differences, they decided to **break off** their engagement.*

*Despite efforts to salvage the negotiation, they had to **break off** talks without reaching an agreement.*

*The climbers were forced to **break off** their ascent due to adverse weather conditions.*

*It's important to know when to **break off** a conversation to avoid unnecessary conflict.*

Come off

To detach or be removed from a surface; to be successful or achieve the desired result.

*The sticker wouldn't **come off** easily, requiring some effort to peel it away.*

*Despite the challenges, the event managed to **come off** as a great success.*

*She was worried that her plan wouldn't **come off**, but everything went according to schedule.*

*With the right strategy, the marketing campaign is likely to **come off** effectively.*

*It's important to have a backup plan in case the original idea doesn't **come off** as expected.*

Back out

To withdraw or retract from a commitment, promise, or agreement; to decline or cancel participation.

*He had initially agreed to help, but at the last minute, he decided to **back out** of the project.*

*Despite the prior commitment, she had to **back out** of attending the event due to an emergency.*

*It's not fair to **back out** of a deal after both parties have reached an agreement.*

*They were disappointed when their friend had to **back out** of the road trip due to unforeseen circumstances.*

*Before committing to anything, it's important to consider the implications and not hastily **back out**.*

Call out

To shout or say something loudly; to publicly criticize or challenge someone or something.

*She had to **call out** to get the attention of her friend across the crowded room.*

*Employees were encouraged to **call out** any unethical behavior within the organization.*

*During the protest, the demonstrators would **call out** slogans demanding justice.*

*It's important to **call out** discriminatory practices and work towards creating an inclusive environment.*

*When you witness wrongdoing, don't hesitate to **call out** the behavior and stand up for what is* *right.*

Clear out

To remove or empty the contents of a space; to evacuate or leave a place quickly.

*Before the renovation, they needed to **clear out** the furniture from the living room.*

*Upon hearing the fire alarm, residents were instructed to **clear out** of the building immediately.*

*It's time to **clear out** the old files and make room for the new documents in the office.*

*After the event, volunteers worked to **clear out** the venue and restore it to its original condition.*

*They decided to **clear out** the clutter in the garage to create more storage space.*

Die out

To become extinct or cease to exist; to fade away gradually.

*Unfortunately, many endangered species are at risk of **dying out** if conservation efforts are not intensified.*

*Traditional practices and customs can **die out** over time if not passed down to the next generation.*

*As technology advances, some old forms of communication may **die out** in favor of more modern methods.*

*If the company doesn't adapt to market changes, it could **die out** over the next few years.*

*Language diversity is essential to prevent certain languages from **dying out** and losing their cultural significance.*

Fall out

To have a disagreement or argument; to drop or come loose from a position.

*As a natural part of aging, some individuals may experience hair starting to **fall out**.*

*When the building caught fire, several windows began to **fall out** due to the intense heat.*

*It's a common experience for children to have their baby teeth **fall out**, making way for the permanent ones.*

*The decision to relocate the factory caused many employees to **fall out** with the management.*

Farm out

To contract, delegate, or outsource work, tasks, or responsibilities to others.

*Due to the high demand, the company decided to **farm out** some of its production to a specialized facility.*

*Instead of hiring additional staff, they chose to **farm out** certain tasks to freelancers.*

*During the busy season, they often need to **farm out** some of the orders to other manufacturers.*

*Parents may choose to **farm out** childcare responsibilities to trusted relatives or babysitters.*

Hear out

To listen to someone's perspective, concerns, or ideas without interruption; to give someone an opportunity to express themselves fully.

*Before making a decision, it's important to **hear out** all stakeholders and consider their input.*

*When conflicts arise, leaders should aim to **hear out** both sides before reaching a resolution.*

*Even if you disagree, it's essential to **hear out** the other person's viewpoint to foster open communication.*

*During the meeting, everyone was given a chance to **hear out** their colleagues and share their thoughts.*

*Friends should be willing to **hear out** each other during challenging times and offer support.*

Help out

To assist or aid someone; to provide support or assistance.

*When the neighbor was sick, the community rallied together to **help out** with daily tasks.*

*Volunteers regularly **help out** at the local shelter by providing meals and assistance to those in need.*

*Family members often **help out** each other during challenging times to ease the burden.*

*During the event, many people came forward to **help out** with organizing and managing the activities.*

*It's always appreciated when colleagues are willing to **help out** with additional work to meet deadlines.*

Leave out

To omit or exclude something or someone; to not include or mention.

*When writing the report, be careful not to **leave out** any crucial details.*

*During the selection process, it's important not to **leave out** any qualified candidates.*

*She accidentally **left out** a key ingredient from the recipe, affecting the final dish.*

*It's not fair to **leave out** certain team members when distributing important information.*

*When summarizing the events, try not to **leave out** any significant occurrences.*

Miss out on

To fail to experience or take advantage of an opportunity; to be deprived of something enjoyable or beneficial.

*Don't **miss out on** the chance to attend the conference; it could be a valuable learning experience.*

*She regretted having to **miss out on** the vacation due to work commitments.*

*If you skip the workshop, you might **miss out on** important insights and skills.*

*By staying indoors, you may **miss out on** the beautiful scenery and fresh air outside.*

Sort out

To organize or resolve a situation; to categorize or arrange things systematically.

> They needed to **sort out** the issues within the team to improve collaboration.

> Before the move, it's crucial to **sort out** your belongings and decide what to keep or discard.

> Parents often have to **sort out** conflicts between siblings to maintain a harmonious household.

> The project manager was determined to **sort out** the delays and ensure the project stayed on schedule.

> When faced with a problem, it's important to take the time to **sort out** the details before finding a solution.

Speak out

To express one's opinions, beliefs, or concerns openly and publicly; to advocate for a cause.

> It's important to **speak out** against injustice and discrimination in any form.

> Employees were encouraged to **speak out** about

any workplace issues during the open forum.

*Students organized a protest to **speak out** against environmental degradation and climate change.*

*He decided to **speak out** against the unfair policies that affected the community.*

*People should feel empowered to **speak out** when they witness wrongdoing or unethical behavior.*

Block up

To obstruct or close a passage or opening; to become clogged or congested.

*The fallen tree **blocked up** the road, causing a traffic jam.*

*Over time, the accumulation of debris can **block up** the drainage system.*

*During the construction, they had to **block up** certain entrances for safety reasons.*

*It's important to regularly clean the gutters to prevent them from **blocking up**.*

*When the sewer pipes **block up**, it can lead to*

plumbing issues in the entire neighborhood.

Brighten up

To become happier or more cheerful; to add color or light to a place or situation.

> *His mood began to **brighten up** after receiving positive news about the project.*

> *The garden **brightened up** with the blooming flowers in the spring.*

> *Playing lively music can **brighten up** the atmosphere of a party or gathering.*

> *Her face **brightened up** with a smile when she saw her old friends at the reunion.*

> *Adding vibrant artwork to the walls can **brighten up** a dull or plain room.*

Burn up

To be completely destroyed by fire.

> *The old wooden house began to **burn up** within*

minutes due to the intense flames.

*They had to evacuate the area as the wildfire threatened to **burn up** everything in its path.*

*It's crucial to use fire-resistant materials to prevent structures from easily **burning up** during a fire.*

*During the summer, dry vegetation can easily **burn up** in the hot sun.*

Call up

To contact someone by phone; to summon or evoke a memory or emotion.

*She decided to **call up** her friend to invite them to the event.*

*If you have any questions, feel free to **call up** our customer service hotline for assistance.*

*The photograph **called up** memories of their childhood spent together.*

*Listening to the song **called up** emotions from a time long ago.*

*During the emergency, it's essential to **call up** the appropriate authorities for help.*

Check up on

To inquire about someone or something, typically to ensure that everything is okay or to get updated information.

*Before a long road trip, it's advisable to **check up on** the car's oil, brakes, and tires.*

*After being sick for a week, Mary's friend decided to **check up on** her to see how she was feeling.*

*After the surgery, the nurse will **check up on** the patient to monitor their recovery.*

*The project manager decided to **check up on** the team's progress to make sure they were meeting their deadlines.*

Chop up

To cut something into smaller pieces, typically using a knife or similar tool.

*She had to **chop up** vegetables for the stir-fry.*

*Before cooking, it's necessary to **chop up** the ingredients into manageable pieces.*

*The chef skillfully **chopped up** the herbs to garnish the dish.*

*They decided to **chop up** the fallen tree for firewood.*

*For the salad, it's best to **chop up** the lettuce and other fresh vegetables.*

Close up

To shut or seal something completely; to approach or move nearer; to end or conclude.

*Before leaving, make sure to **close up** all the windows and doors.*

*The photographer decided to **close up** on the subject to capture detailed shots.*

*As the store was closing, the employees began to **close up** the registers.*

*The meeting will officially **close up** with a summary of key points and action items.*

*After the event, it's essential to **close up** the venue and secure any remaining equipment.*

Crack up

To break or fracture into pieces; to burst into laughter; to suffer a mental or emotional breakdown.

*The old vase accidentally **cracked up** when it fell off the shelf.*

*The comedian's joke made the entire audience **crack up** with laughter.*

*The intense stress caused him to **crack up** emotionally, leading to a period of self-reflection and recovery.*

*It's important to find healthy ways to cope with stress and avoid **cracking up** under pressure.*

Do up

To fasten or secure something; to renovate or

decorate; to wrap or package; to complete or finish a task; to preserve or process food items for future use.

*She had to **do up** her shoelaces before going for a run.*

*Before the party, they decided to **do up** the house with festive decorations.*

*It's essential to **do up** the seatbelt for safety while driving.*

*He carefully **did up** the birthday present with colorful wrapping paper.*

*Before leaving, make sure to **do up** the buttons on your coat to stay warm.*

*I need to **do up** this report before the meeting tomorrow.*

*Yesterday, I **did up** a batch of homemade pickles from the cucumbers in my garden.*

Dress up

To wear formal or stylish clothing; to put on special attire for a specific occasion.

*They decided to **dress up** in elegant outfits for the anniversary celebration.*

*Children often enjoy **dressing up** in costumes for Halloween.*

*It's a formal event, so make sure to **dress up** in a suit and tie.*

*She likes to **dress up** in colorful clothes to express her unique style.*

*Despite the casual nature of the gathering, he chose to **dress up** to make a good impression.*

Eat up

To consume all the food that is served; to finish eating.

*Children, make sure to **eat up** your vegetables before having dessert.*

*Despite being full, he encouraged her to **eat up** the delicious homemade meal.*

*It's polite to **eat up** when you're a guest at someone's house.*

She couldn't resist the tasty dish and decided to ***eat up*** *every bite.*

During the picnic, everyone was encouraged to ***eat up*** *the sandwiches and snacks.*

Go up

To increase in height, value, or quantity; to ascend or move upward.

The cost of living tends to ***go up*** *over time.*

They watched the hot air balloon ***go up*** *into the sky.*

After the successful product launch, stock prices began to ***go up***.

As you ***go up*** *the mountain, the air becomes thinner.*

Real estate prices in the city continue to ***go up*** *due to high demand.*

Fix up

To repair, improve, or renovate something; to arrange or organize.

*They decided to **fix up** the old house and turn it into a cozy cottage.*

*Before selling the car, they needed to **fix up** the engine and repaint it.*

*He promised to **fix up** the backyard and create a beautiful garden.*

*It's time to **fix up** the website to make it more user-friendly.*

*Before the guests arrive, let's **fix up** the living room and make it presentable.*

Hold up

To support or bear the weight of something; to delay or hinder; to withstand or endure.

*The sturdy columns **hold up** the roof of the ancient temple.*

*Unexpected road repairs may **hold up** the progress of the construction project.*

*She managed to **hold up** the heavy box until someone could assist her.*

*Despite the challenges, the team was determined to **hold up** under pressure.*

*During the storm, the old house continued to **hold up** despite strong winds.*

Hurry up

To move or act quickly; to accelerate the pace of an activity.

*We need to **hurry up** if we want to catch the train.*

*Don't forget to **hurry up** so we can make it to the appointment on time.*

*If you **hurry up** with the preparations, we can leave earlier for the event.*

*Students were urged to **hurry up** and submit their assignments before the deadline.*

*As the deadline approaches, it's essential to **hurry up** and complete the project.*

Keep up

To maintain pace or progress; to continue at the same rate; to stay informed or be aware.

*It's challenging to **keep up** with the fast pace of the competitive industry.*

*Don't worry; you can **keep up** with the group during the hike.*

*It's important to **keep up** with industry trends to remain competitive.*

*Make sure to **keep up** with your assignments to avoid falling behind in class.*

*She reads the news daily to **keep up** with current events.*

Screw up

To make a serious mistake or error; to mess up or mishandle a situation.

*I didn't mean to **screw up** the presentation; it was a technical glitch.*

It's essential to double-check the details to avoid

__screwing up__ the important document.

She felt terrible after realizing she had __screwed up__ the dinner reservations.

Try not to __screw up__ the project by missing the key deadlines.

Apologize if you __screw up__ and take responsibility for your actions.

Warm up

To increase in temperature; to prepare the body for physical activity through gentle exercises.

Before the race, athletes engage in stretching exercises to __warm up__ their muscles.

During winter, it takes a while for the car engine to __warm up__ in the cold weather.

It's advisable to __warm up__ before lifting heavy weights to prevent injuries.

Before the performance, the singer takes time to __warm up__ her vocal cords.

Before the soccer match, players gather to __warm__

up and practice drills.

Wake up

To rouse from sleep; to become alert or aware; to acknowledge a fact or reality.

*Every morning, the alarm clock helps him **wake up** and start the day.*

*It's time to **wake up** to the importance of environmental conservation.*

*She tried to **wake up** her brother gently without disturbing his sleep.*

*After a deep sleep, it can take a moment to fully **wake up** and be aware of surroundings.*

*It's crucial to **wake up** to the realities of social issues and work towards positive change.*

Go along with

To agree with or support; to follow or accompany.

*He decided to **go along with** the team's decision*

even though he had reservations.

*If everyone **goes along with** the plan, we can successfully complete the project.*

*I'm planning a road trip next week, and I was wondering if you'd like to **go along with** me.*

Grind along

To continue making slow and steady progress; to persist despite challenges.

*Despite the setbacks, the team decided to **grind along** and work towards their goals.*

*It may be tough, but we need to **grind along** and overcome the obstacles in our path.*

*Entrepreneurs often have to **grind along** in the early stages of building a business.*

*Even when faced with adversity, it's important to **grind along** and stay focused on the long-term objectives.*

*They were determined to **grind along** and achieve success through hard work and dedication.*

Happen along

To come across or encounter by chance; to find or discover unexpectedly.

*As they explored the forest, they **happened along** a hidden waterfall.*

*While strolling through the antique market, she **happened along** a rare and valuable item.*

*They didn't plan to find anything, but they **happened along** an interesting book in the library.*

*During the road trip, they often **happened along** charming little towns with unique attractions.*

*As they were walking on the beach, they **happened along** a collection of seashells.*

Move along

To proceed, progress, or continue moving.

*After a brief stop, it's time to **move along** and continue our journey.*

*The traffic officer gestured for the cars to **move***

Muddle along

To proceed or move forward in a confused or disorganized manner, often without a clear plan or direction.

Pass along

To transmit or convey something to others; to hand or transfer something from one person to another.

> She decided to **pass along** the valuable advice her mentor had given her.

> As a tradition, they would **pass along** family heirlooms to the next generation.

> It's important to **pass along** knowledge and skills to foster continuous learning.

> During the meeting, the CEO encouraged managers to **pass along** important updates to their teams.

Play along

To participate in a situation or activity, often by pretending or cooperating.

> Even though she knew it was a joke, she decided to **play along** with their prank.

> He agreed to **play along** with the surprise party, pretending not to know about it.

*It's important for team members to **play along** with the collaborative spirit and contribute ideas.*

*Children often enjoy imaginative games where they **play along** with different roles and scenarios.*

Run along

To depart or leave quickly; to continue on one's way.

*After delivering the message, he told the messenger to **run along**.*

*Children, it's time to finish your homework and then you can **run along** and play.*

*She waved goodbye and asked him to **run along** to catch the bus.*

*Once the task is complete, feel free to **run along** and enjoy the rest of your day.*

*After the meeting, they were given permission to **run along** and attend to their other commitments.*

String along

To deceive or mislead someone, often by providing false hope or promises.

> *He realized that the smooth-talking salesman was trying to **string him along** with unrealistic expectations.*
>
> *Don't let someone **string you along** with empty promises; seek clarity and honesty.*
>
> *She decided to end the relationship when she realized he was just **stringing her along**.*

Tag along

To accompany or follow someone, often without a specific invitation.

> *A few friends are going to the beach. Can I **tag along** with them?*
>
> *She asked if she could **tag along** to the bookstore with her friends.*
>
> *Feeling lonely, she asked if she could **tag along** with the group going to the movies.*

Take along

To bring or carry someone or something along on a journey or outing.

> *When going to the beach, don't forget to **take along** sunscreen and snacks.*

> *She decided to **take her dog along** for a walk in the park.*

> *They planned to **take along** a picnic basket for a day in the countryside.*

> *He offered to **take along** his camera to capture memories during the road trip.*

Trundle along

To move slowly and steadily.

> *The old wagon began to **trundle along** the dirt road pulled by a horse.*

> *As the baby learned to walk, they watched him **trundle along** unsteadily.*

> *Despite the heavy load, the delivery cart continued to **trundle along** the cobblestone*

street.

*The toddler giggled with delight as the toy train **trundled along** the tracks.*

Be along

To arrive or come; to appear or join at a particular time.

*He mentioned that he would **be along** shortly after finishing his work.*

*Don't start the game without me; I'll **be along** in a few minutes.*

*She assured them that she would **be along** for the family dinner despite being late.*

*After completing the errands, he promised to **be along** for the gathering at the park.*

*As soon as the meeting concludes, I'll **be along** to discuss the project with you.*

Stroll through

To walk in a relaxed and leisurely manner, especially
while exploring an area.

*On weekends, they like to **stroll through** the
neighborhood and discover new cafes.*

*Visitors often **stroll through** the historic district,
enjoying the architecture and ambiance.*

*She decided to take a break and **stroll through**
the park to clear her mind.*

*During vacations, they love to **stroll through**
local markets and immerse themselves in the
culture.*

*Before dinner, they took a delightful **stroll
through** the garden to enjoy the evening breeze.*

Plonk down

To casually or heavily place or drop something.

*After a long day at work, he decided to **plonk
down** on the couch and relax.*

*She grabbed a book and **plonked it down** on the
table before joining the conversation.*

*Feeling exhausted, they **plonked themselves down** at the picnic table for a quick break.*

*He entered the room and **plonked** his bag **down** on the floor with a sigh.*

*Before starting the meeting, she **plonked down** a stack of papers for everyone to review.*

Curse out

To verbally express strong disapproval, anger, or frustration towards someone; to use offensive language or curse words.

*He was so frustrated with the situation that he decided to **curse out** the person responsible.*

*It's not appropriate to **curse out** your colleagues, even in challenging situations.*

*She regretted her decision to **curse out** her friend during the argument.*

*Instead of **cursing out** the customer, the service representative remained calm and addressed the issue professionally.*

*When angered, it's important to find constructive ways to communicate rather than resorting to **cursing out** others.*

Run by

To present or inform someone about an idea, plan, or proposal; to seek approval or feedback.

*Before implementing the changes, he decided to **run them by** the team for input.*

*She always makes sure to **run her ideas by** her supervisor before initiating any new projects.*

*It's a good practice to **run potential solutions by** the stakeholders to ensure alignment.*

*Before finalizing the budget, it's essential to **run it by** the finance committee for approval.*

*He wanted to **run the proposal by** his peers before presenting it to the management team.*

Pass away

To die or cease to exist; a euphemistic expression for

death.

*It was a sad day when their beloved pet **passed away** after many years of companionship.*

*He **passed away** peacefully in his sleep, surrounded by his loved ones.*

*After a long illness, she finally **passed away**, leaving a void in the hearts of her family and friends.*

*The community mourned when the respected elder **passed away** at the age of 90.*

*Although he **passed away**, his legacy continued through the impact he had on others.*

Act up

To behave disruptively or improperly; to malfunction or not work correctly; to display erratic behavior.

*Children tend to **act up** when they are tired or bored.*

*The computer started to **act up** after the software update, causing delays in the work.*

*It's crucial to address any issues when electronic devices begin to **act up** to prevent further damage.*

*During the performance, the microphone began to **act up**, creating challenges for the speaker.*

*If your car starts to **act up**, it's advisable to have it checked by a mechanic.*

Big up

To praise, commend, or express admiration for someone or something; to give recognition or acclaim.

*It's important to **big up** individuals who contribute significantly to the success of the team.*

*She took a moment to **big up** her colleagues for their hard work and dedication.*

*At the awards ceremony, they took the opportunity to **big up** the volunteers for their invaluable contributions.*